STENCILING

MEGAN PARRY

VNR VAN NOSTRAND REINHOLD COMPANY
New York Cincinnati Toronto London Melbourne

TO BEN AND STEPHANIE

WITH PHOTOGRAPHS BY LESLEY BRILL

Copyright © 1977 by Litton Educational Publishing, Inc.
Library of Congress Catalog Card Number 76-56541
ISBN 0-442-21055-8

Printed in United States of America
Designed by Loudan Enterprise

Published in 1977 by Van Nostrand Reinhold Company
A Division of Litton Educational Publishing, Inc.
450 West 33rd Street
New York, NY 10001, U.S.A.

Van Nostrand Reinhold Limited
1410 Birchmount Road
Scarborough, Ontario M1P 2E7, Canada

Van Nostrand Reinhold Australia Pty. Ltd.
17 Queen Street
Mitcham, Victoria 3132, Australia

Van Nostrand Reinhold Company Ltd.
Molly Millars Land
Wokingham, Berkshire, England

16 15 14 13 12 11 10 9 8 7 6 5 4 3 2

Library of Congress Cataloging in Publication Data

Parry, Megan.
  Stenciling.

  Includes index.
  1. Stencil work.   I. Title.
TT270.P37   745.7'3   76-56541
ISBN 0-442-21055-8

CONTENTS

Chapter 1: **ABOUT STENCILING**   5

Chapter 2: **MAKING STENCILS**   11

Chapter 3: **INVENTING AND DISCOVERING DESIGNS**   29

Chapter 4: **PLANNING A ROOM**   61

Chapter 5: **WALL STENCILING**   79

Chapter 6: **PROJECTS**   93

Chapter 7: **FULL-SIZE DESIGNS FOR TRACING**   111

INDEX   135

Plate 1. Model room, May D & F, Denver, Colorado.

CHAPTER 1:

ABOUT STENCILING

I've been stenciling for five years. When I first began, I knew no one else who was doing it. Now my colleagues have increased to the extent that I need only open the nearest house-and-home magazine to find an example of stenciling in a modern setting. Besides reflecting the current enthusiasm for the handmade, the stenciling revival introduces personalization and craftsmanship into what is very often an impersonal setting—the twentieth-century contractor-designed home. In the eighteenth and nineteenth centuries stenciling gave color and individuality to the simple, bare rooms of American farmhouses. In the twentieth century, while designers avert their eyes and attention, homeowners face a similar lack of distinction in their suburban (or urban) tract houses.

The stenciling tradition is international. It belongs to many cultures and all periods. Stenciling is probably the easiest way to repeat an image accurately, and without repetition there would be no pattern or design. It isn't surprising that stenciling is popular wherever people make designs. And the universality of stencil designing appeals to any culture that spends as much time as we do searching out this rug from India, that Japanese teapot, and these fabrics from Guatemala to enliven modern interiors.

Plate 2. Living room, Boulder, Colorado.

Plate 3. Kitchen, Vail, Colorado.

Plate 4. Bedroom, Boulder, Colorado.

Stenciling attained its greatest popularity in the United States in the period shortly after the Revolution until the mid-nineteenth century. It served as a substitute for costly imported wallpapers and finally declined when American machines began to print wallpaper that was cheap enough for middle-class Americans. Before that awful day, however, many an itinerant interior decorator earned his keep by roaming through New England and beyond painting walls wherever he went. It is claimed (little is known for certain about these artists and their business arrangements) that they usually traded their product for dry goods and even for unadulterated bed and board.

They must have traveled light, since they did not need much equipment. They carried dry pigments, which were mixed with the skim-milk medium provided by any farm; brushes; paper or leather for stencils; a knife for cutting; and/or a basic repertoire of ready-cut designs. Some probably carried measuring devices (a chalk line or plumb bob), but adequate measurements can be made with a stick, and the work of many early stencilers reveals a flamboyant, often charming disregard for precision in measuring. After engaging the interest of the consumer (with funny stories or card tricks?) the stenciler would display his design repertoire. Some old stenciling survives only in attic stairways in the form of sample renderings in varying colors.

If stencilers traveled alone, inventing designs and repeating favorites, it would follow that some developed individual styles and that we might trace their progress cross-country through the remnants of stenciled walls that still exist today. This seems to be the case: the careers of Jared Jessop and Moses Eaton emerge from obscurity thanks partly to Jessop's distinctive combination of hand painting with stenciling and to Eaton's reliance on a personal vocabulary of original designs. The fact that Jessop occasionally signed his work (an eccentricity at that time) and that Eaton's stencils were preserved in an attic were additional aids to identification. Scholars such as Janet Waring and Jean Lipman deserve credit for discovering the work of many old-time artists.

Naturally enough, stencil designs tended to imitate the coveted wallpaper motifs. They also reflected such post-Revolutionary enthusiasms as patriotism. Drapery flounces, American eagles with stars, pineapples, willow trees, horses, vines, and geometrical figures all appeared regularly on walls, often in incongruous juxtaposition. Later designs (early to mid–1800s) favored Greek motifs borrowed from contemporary architecture, furniture design, and wallpaper. The collective work of almost a century forms the tradition of American stenciling. Many sites in New England and New York State have preserved representative stenciling designs and are well worth visiting. Historic Deerfield and Sturbridge Village in Massachusetts, the Shelburne Museum in Vermont, and the restored town Mumford near Rochester, New York all display interesting and beautiful examples of stenciled rooms.

After 1850 the freely measured and whimsically planned stencil decoration of earlier times vanished under layers of the now widely available status symbol. As an accompaniment to the new wallpaper, however, a contemporary stenciling style evolved, which prevailed throughout the Victorian period. The designs consisted almost entirely of borders, borrowed heavily from Greek treatments of foliage and floral forms. Border arrangements of these elements commonly ran around the top of a wall, next to the ceiling, and above the wallpaper. Stenciling often appeared on curved molding, since wallpaper would not have adhered properly. Stenciling on other wood surfaces (doors, the perimeter of a floor, even wainscoting) was also common.

Oddly enough, the technical peak of American stencil art was yet to occur. Around the turn of the nineteenth century stenciling dropped out of favor with the middle class but became a decorating tool of such designers and architects as Louis C. Tiffany and Louis Sullivan. The styles that they developed and worked in were consciously eclectic, with forms and colors evoking a wildly international potpourri of exotic sources.

Plate 5. Turn-of-the-century border, Denver, Colorado.

The most dominant influences were probably the complex and airy geometry of Islamic design and pre–Raphaelite Gothicism—poured into the art-nouveau mold and intermixed with hints of China, Japan, and India. Some early twentieth-century examples used many stencils to produce an unprecedented number of colors and shades—and the stencils themselves were intricately cut and carefully designed for perfect synchronization. The old slapdashery and bright, simple colors had entirely disappeared. Early twentieth-century designers followed the dictates of art nouveau and William Morris's arts-and-crafts movement. They chose rich, subtle blends of colors—muted shades of rose, olive, ocher, camel, and turquoise, often highlighted with metallic pigments of gold, copper, and silver.

The Mark Twain Memorial in Hartford, Connecticut displays richly decorated rooms by Louis Tiffany and Associated Artists. The Chicago Art Institute owns a Louis Sullivan panel, Islamic in influence, that once accompanied others like it in the foyer of one of his buildings. In Denver an important example of turn-of-the-century stenciling exists in a near-perfect state of preservation at the house inhabited by the executive offices of the Denver Botanical Gardens. The most subtly colorful and complicated stenciling that I've ever seen appears on the ceiling of a large reception hall. Although it has a definitely oriental quality, the colors, composition, and stylization of forms place it firmly within the art-nouveau tradition. The rest of the stenciling, in accord with the fanciful architecture, evokes Islamic art (with a strong suggestion of art

Plate 6. Entrance hall, Mark Twain Memorial, Hartford, Connecticut.

deco). The taste for such high-powered visual thrills has not reached a comparable dimension since the onset of the depression. Even wallpaper has declined in popularity, partially superseded by the solid colors of interior latex—cheap, easy to apply, and easy to replace.

Today many of us live in homes that were built since World War II. Our walls are bare of decorative plaster molding; the framing around both windows and doors is a simple curve measuring a modest 2¼" (5.7 cm) in width, and the same trim lines the baseboard. No gracefully carved wood or plaster celebrates the meeting of the wall with the ceiling. Our windows and doors look like everyone else's; even our floor plans match. The cost of construction materials and labor forbids architectural flights of fancy and encourages visual conformity. In many ways our situation resembles that of the American colonists, who, although basic building materials occurred in plentiful supply, had neither the means nor the time to produce or import superfluous decoration for ordinary houses. The early stenciler fit neatly into these circumstances. He probably demanded little cash payment for his labor, and his work required no time at all from the owner of the house. Most, though not all, of the homes decorated by stencilers were plain town- or farmhouses. Like the tract houses of today, they contained no extravagant woodwork or fancy plaster geometry.

Stenciled designs and colors brought distinction and charm to these simple houses. I will be pleased if this book helps someone restore a beautiful period home, but I want most to address the majority who live in houses that, though pleasant and comfortable, have little intrinsic distinction and who feel the need and desire to make them more interesting in an unusual, personal way.

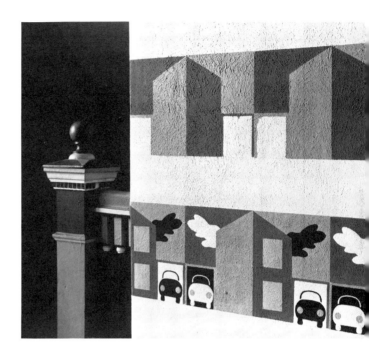

Plate 8. Stenciling in progress, Boulder, Colorado.

Plate 7. Ceiling, Denver Botanic Gardens.

Plate 9. Hall, Mark Twain Memorial, Hartford,
Connecticut.

CHAPTER 2:

MAKING STENCILS

BASIC DESIGN

You can make a stencil right now. You need nothing more than a grocery bag (for stencil paper), a section of the Sunday paper, a pencil, a small paintbrush, water-based paint, a pair of scissors, and some blank newsprint (art-supply stores sell it in big tablets) or any other big, light-colored paper, such as brown wrapping paper.

Cut a piece of grocery-bag paper about 8″ × 8″ (21 × 21 cm) square. Fold it in half and draw half the body of a person at the fold (fig. 2-1). Keep the paper folded and cut out the shape with scissors. When you open the paper, you'll have a negative paper doll—all hole, no substance (fig. 2-2). Whatever its flaws may be, the design is perfectly symmetrical—and it's a stencil.

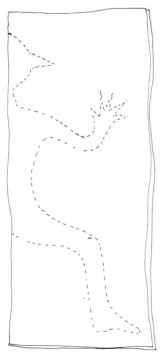

2-1.

2-2.

Spread out a big sheet of blank paper—newsprint or whatever—and, using a small brush and any kind of water-based paint, paint the stencil design on the paper, holding the stencil as flat as possible. Use only small amounts of paint on the brush. The paint should have a pea-soup texture: if it's too thick, add some water. Brush away from the sides of the stencil towards the middle of the design. Don't let the brush bump against the sides of the stencil. When the open area is completely covered with paint, lift the stencil and have a look. Don't be too critical at this point: the paint may have seeped around the edges of the design, and the color may be so transparent that you can see every brush stroke. These flaws result from the equipment—you're working under the most primitive conditions known to man! You *can* make stencils in this

2-3.

way, however, and you could decorate whole towns with them. Everything else from here on is just refinement.

Paint many versions of your stencil on a big piece of paper. When the stencil becomes too soggy to hold together, make a few more. Line the little people up into horizontal and vertical rows; see how they work in borders and stripes. Arrange the design in groups of three and four; stencil it upside down; make a border in which every other design is upside down. Make the figures hold hands by overlapping the stencil slightly; make them stand on each other's heads; stencil them with their feet together, casting reflections of one another (fig. 2-3). Wipe the stencils with tissue paper or with your fingers after each application. Paint eventually builds up on the back, and the images will become progressively sloppier.

The finished sheet, completely covered with little stenciled people, makes a nice piece of wrapping paper. Or you could cut out the nicest parts and write letters to your friends on the backs. Whatever you do, you have learned how to make a stencil, how to paint with it, and how to arrange it into designs.

COMPLICATED STENCILS

Now that you're really into stencil-making, you need some new tools, all inexpensive and easily obtainable from an art-supply store. Get an X-acto knife—I like the smaller, pen-sized version—with #16 blades. If this size is not available, get #11 blades, which are almost as good. You also need oiled stencil board, which is heavy and stiff: don't get flimsy, tissuey stencil paper. If the store doesn't have oiled stencil board, get bristol board, which is smooth, heavy, and stiff enough and comes in pads or big sheets. You should get a metal yardstick and a knife sharpener or a piece of Carborundum to sharpen your X-acto blades. I use a common kitchen knife sharpener that has two rows of little metal spinning disks. If you don't want to be bothered, you can throw away the blades as you wear them out—I did this for years, sometimes at the rate of two or three per hour. It was painless. Buy a good brush, about ½" (12.7 mm) wide, made for painting with acrylics. It has a long handle and flat, soft, square-cut bristles. Get some acrylic paint as well—it comes in 2-ounce (59 ml) tubes (fig. 2-4).

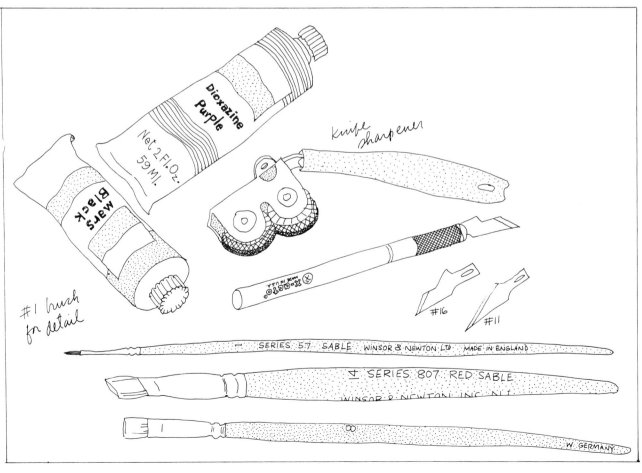

2-4.

The first part of stencil making is to draw the design on the stencil board. Which method to use depends largely on the type of design. The easy design (fig. 2-2) was bilaterally symmetrical—made by folding a piece of paper in half. A radially symmetrical design is more complicated. It consists of four quadrants, all of which match. Eight- and four-pointed stars are radially symmetrical, as are many early American and Victorian designs. To learn the technique, use the design shown in fig. 2-5 as an example. You don't have to like it— it's just for practice.

Say that the design measures 4″ × 4″ (10.5 × 10.5 cm). Since radial symmetry requires a lot of folding, use a piece of plain white paper instead of a heavy grocery bag. Cut it down to 6″ (15.5 cm) square. Fold the paper in half (fig. 2-6). Fold it in half again, turning the rectangle into a square (fig. 2-7). Fold it into a triangle (fig. 2-8) and put it aside. Draw a line that bisects the design (fig. 2-5) from top to bottom and from side to side. Draw two diagonal lines that run from corner to corner, passing through the center of the design (fig. 2-9). The design is now divided into eighths. Draw one-eighth of the design on the little paper triangle (fig. 2-10).

To cut out the design, place the folded-paper triangle on top of one or two sections of newspaper and hold it as flat and steady as possible. Holding your knife perpendicular, cut the paper as if you were drawing in an especially deliberate way. Bear down hard enough to penetrate all the layers at the same time. To turn corners, turn the paper, not the knife.

2-5.

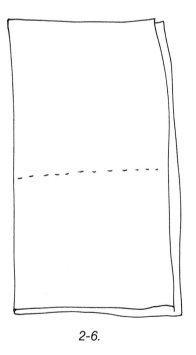

2-6.

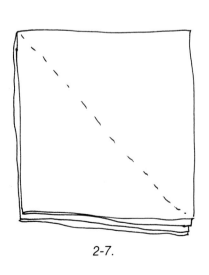

2-7.

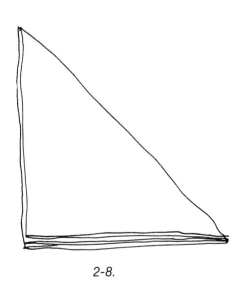

2-8.

Always turn the paper so that, if you're right-handed, the knife moves toward your right elbow. You may have to go over the corners more than once: it can be tricky to make cuts meet precisely in corners. If you don't penetrate all the layers, go over the cuts carefully until you do. When you're through cutting, unfold the paper. You will have a perfectly symmetrical replica of the design. Trace it onto stencil board, using the edges of the cutout to guide your pencil.

If you're in the mood, make some paper-cutout variations on the design. Try elongating the arms, curling the points, and even adding extra parts if you want to. If you're really in the mood, fold and cut the paper to make random geometrical figures. Try them out on a big sheet of newsprint (fig. 2-11), as with the paper doll (fig. 2-3).

Suppose the design that you want to transfer to stencil board is not the least bit symmetrical. If it's the right size, use tracing paper to make a replica and transfer the design from the tracing paper to stencil board with carbon paper. Put the carbon paper face-down on the stencil board, and the tracing paper over the carbon paper. Make sure that all three are lined up and, holding them as steady as rocks, redraw the outlines of the design.

If the design is the wrong size for a direct tracing, you'll need some graph paper and graph tracing paper. Original designs are more apt to be too small than too big, so you should get graph tracing paper with smaller squares (five to the inch, perhaps) than the usual (four

squares per inch). Trace the design directly on the graph tracing paper and redraw, square by square, on the plain graph paper. If the scale is still wrong, you can either try graph paper with more or fewer squares per inch or make your own graph paper with the proper-size squares by drawing a grid on plain paper. The square-by-square method of drawing designs often leaves them ragged and choppy. Go over them with a heavy line and smooth them out so that they look more graceful. When you're finished, you can transfer the design to stencil board via carbon paper.

If you've tried these methods, you know that some are more accurate than others. Don't become obsessed with precision copying. If you use the folded-paper method, the charm of symmetry will always lend your designs *some* appeal. If you feel that whatever you do is never as nice as the original, use other people's designs in the right size and just trace them.

Cutting stencil board is essentially the same as cutting lighter paper. Try to bevel the edges of the stencil by inclining the knife away from the center of the work: this prevents the paint from blotting under the edges. If you're right-handed, always tilt the knife to the right. Hold the stencil board firmly against the newspaper and turn it regularly so that you can always cut in the same direction. Make sure that the blade is sharp and even, trim any rough edges, and recut any corners that are not as neat as pins. You should be constantly sharpening or throwing away blades during a long stencil-cutting session.

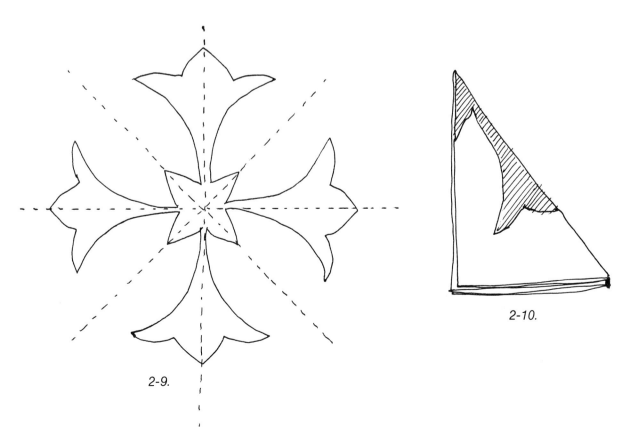

2-9.

2-10.

16

STENCILS WITH TIES

Ties—connecting strips—enable you to make a stencil from a line drawing. Say that you have a simple line drawing of a fish. You cut out the design, and—behold!—the middle falls out, leaving nothing but an outline—no eyes, no scales, no teeth (fig. 2-12). To keep the middle, you have to leave little bridges from the mainland to the island. These bridges, spaces, or ties connect the middle of the stencil with the outside (fig. 2-13). If you stencil the design on the wall, the ties will leave white spaces in the outline. If you don't like them, you can paint over them after you finish stenciling.

Plate 10. Ties and register marks.

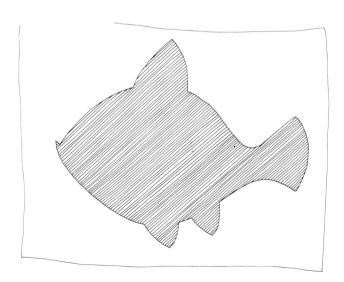

2-12.

2-13.

Ties can also keep colors separate if you use the same stencil to produce a two- or three-color design. If you want your simple stencil (fig. 2-2) to have a blue head and hands, red body, green feet, and yellow hat, for example, cut it out again, leaving little spaces (ties!) between the colors (fig. 2-14).

Ties strengthen weak stencils. A stencil with long, sinuous sections is a weak stencil that tends to warp and buckle. If you make a snake stencil, for example, you have to leave ties (unless it's very short and fat) to keep it sturdy (fig. 2-15). A snake with many regularly spaced ties is a striped snake: many striped or figured designs have such built-in ties (fig. 2-16). The fish stencil (fig. 2-17) has interconnecting scales that function as a series of ties, joining the pattern to the outside of the stencil in an especially ingenious, unobtrusive way. The ties are an important element in the design.

As you make your own stencils, look them over to see if and where they need ties. A vine design, for example, needs a tie between each leaf or flower and the stem. If the stem itself crosses the stencil snake-fashion, it will also need ties (fig. 2-18). When you cut out the design, try to avoid cutting through the ties. If you make a mistake (and you will), repair the cuts on both sides with masking tape. Don't fold the excess tape around the stencil in an effort to finish off the repair: cut it away carefully with an X-acto knife.

2-14.

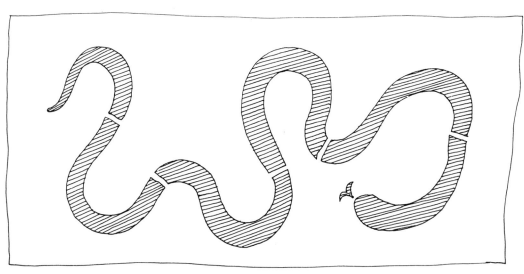

2-15.

2-16.

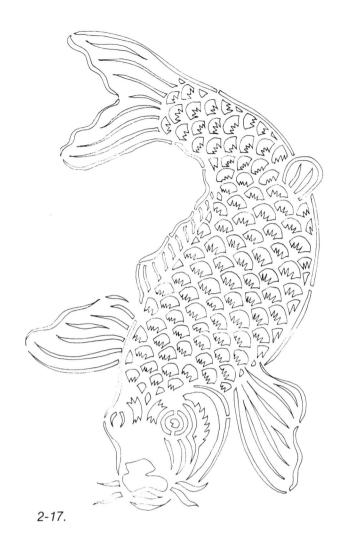

2-17.

2-18.

MULTICOLORED DESIGNS

If you use ties to separate colors in a stencil or if the shapes are far apart, you don't need extra stencils to produce a many-colored design. Take, for example, the familiar blue-headed person: you can use it over and over again, once for each color. The fact that all the colors are visible at the same time makes it easy to position the stencil properly on the wall: to paint the green parts, for example, just fit the blue section of the stencil over the already painted blue area on the wall.

You do, however, need extra stencils for designs in which colors abut or are superimposed on top of one another. Suppose that you have a design that consists of two opposing triangles fitted back to back. One triangle is blue and the other is yellow (fig. 2-19). If the base of each triangle is 3″ (7.8 cm) across, cut two matching 5″-×-5″ (13-×-13 cm) squares of stencil board. Draw one triangle on the first piece and cut it out (fig. 2-20). Place the cutout stencil on top of the second piece of stencil board and line up the edges. Draw the base of the triangle on the new board, using the cut edge of the first stencil as a guide. Remove the cut stencil. Since the triangles come together at their bases, you now know exactly where the second triangle should go. Turn the cut stencil over and place the triangle upside down on the stencil board so that its base coincides with the line drawn on the board. Trace the triangle, using the stencil edges as a guide. Remove the triangle stencil; the triangle drawn on the stencil board should be in exactly the right position (fig. 2-21). Cut it out, leaving the shape the tiniest bit larger than the drawing indicates (fig. 2-22). Tracing from thick stencil board shrinks the image slightly: the extra bit restores it to its proper size.

If the design is asymmetrical (unlike the triangles), the procedure changes. Suppose that the design is a yellow horse with black legs, tail, and mane. The horse is about 6″ (15.5 cm) tall—and long. Cut two matching pieces of stencil board, measuring 8″ × 8″ (21 × 21 cm). Draw the main (yellow) part of the horse's body on one piece and cut it out (fig. 2-23). Position the cutout stencil over the clean stencil board and trace the body of the horse. Now you know exactly where to put the legs and tail on the new stencil. Draw them and cut them out. They should extend into the body section slightly (fig. 2-24) so that the colors abut neatly when you stencil the design.

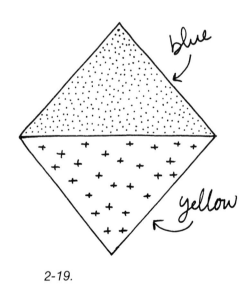

2-19.

2-20.

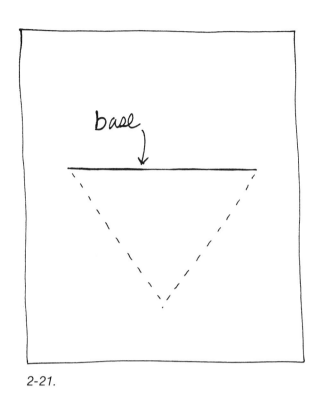

2-21.

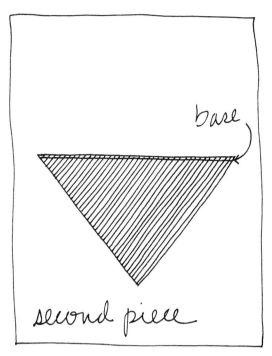

2-22.

2-23.

2-24.

A different procedure is used to superimpose one color over another. Suppose that your design is an oval-shaped blue pool with an orange fish in it. The pool is 4" (10.5 cm) long; the fish, only 1" (2.5 cm) long. The pool is stenciled first, and the fish is stenciled on top of it. Draw the pool on a 4"-×-6" (10.5-×-15.5 cm) piece of stencil board. Cut it out and place it over fresh stencil board of the same size. Draw the outline of the pool, following the cutout edges. Remove the pool stencil and draw the fish in the middle of the traced pool. Draw a series of little triangles along the edge of the traced pool (fig. 2-25). Cut out the fish and the triangles. They indicate the outline of the pool, enabling you to accurately register the fish design over it.

You may want to superimpose detail on a shape—for example, a green snail with red stripes. Draw the outline of the snail on a piece of stencil board and cut it out. Trace the snail's outline on a new piece of stencil board in the usual way. Draw in the stripes and cut them out. Assuming that they extend to the edge of the snail, you don't need register marks. To stencil the stripes on top of the snail, position the stripe stencil so that it fits right over the snail. The stencil is in the right place when no bare wall shows through the stripes (fig. 2-26).

In some cases it is easier to superimpose than to abut colors. Say that your design is a brown house with a black roof and blue windows (fig. 2-27). Though there are three colors, you need only two stencils: one for the house and one for the roof and windows. Draw an outline of the entire house, including the roof, on a piece of stencil board. Cut it out, lay it over a second board; and trace. Draw the windows on the second board and cut them out. Draw the two roofs on the second board and cut them out, making them a little bigger than the drawing indicates so that they will fit properly over the parts of the house that they are supposed to cover. Add a chimney. The two stencils should look like those shown in fig. 2-28. When you do the stenciling, you don't have to worry about lining the stencils up properly. Use the roof lines as a guide for the windows: position them at the edge of the stencil. Superimposing the roof over the house instead of abutting it ensures the cleanest possible contact between colors. With the abutting method the stencils don't always fit perfectly, and little bits of white space may show at the juncture of the colors.

Some colors require you to abut stencils instead of superimposing them. If you want to stencil a light, transparent color such as yellow on top of a cobalt-blue house, you either have to abut the colors or put twenty coats of yellow roof over the blue. Cut the stencils so that the two colors overlap very slightly—less than 1/16" (1.5 mm). This increases your chances of getting a clean edge. The two abutting stencils should look like those shown in fig. 2-29.

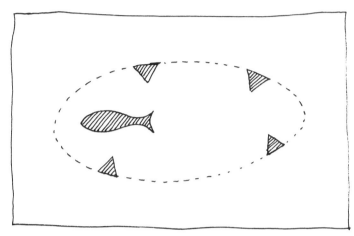

2-25.

2-26.

2-27.

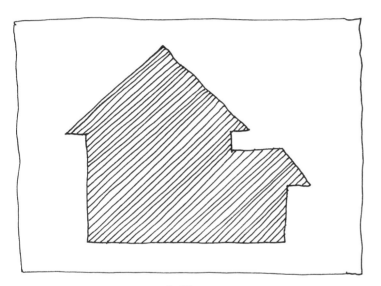

2-28.

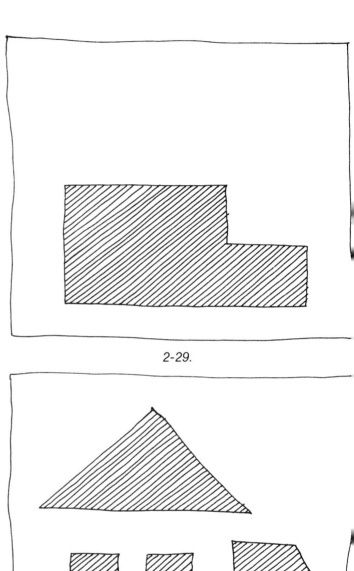

2-29.

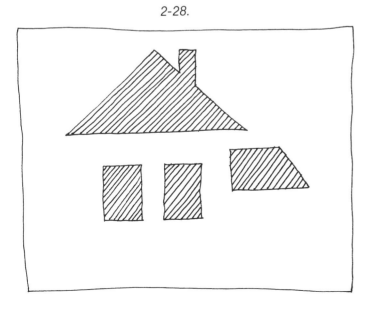

REGISTRATION

The more that the first design is visible through the second stencil, the easier it is to register the latter properly. A good view of the design may be an accidental by-product of the stencil; or you may have to make your own view by cutting windows in the stencil. Always cut them so that they stop at the outline of the first color, as with the fish stencil for the blue pool (fig. 2-25). If your design consists of a green tree with yellow birds in it, for example, you have to make windows in the bird stencil so that you can see where it fits over the tree. Cut little triangles that stop at the edge of the trunk and at the edge of the tree top. Tracing the entire tree on the bird stencil enables you to place the triangles accurately (fig. 2-30).

You may be able to cleverly make the shape of the two stencils the same. For example, if the fish stencil (fig. 2-25) were the same size and shape as the pool, you could simply lay the pool shape, with the fish in it, directly over the painted pool. When the edges of the fish stencil and of the painted pool were in perfect agreement, you could safely stencil the fish (fig. 2-31).

BORDERS AND STRIPES

You could make a border design with a duck stencil by repeating it every 6″ (15.5 cm) or so until your room was ringed with ducks. It's more convenient, however, to arrange the ducks on one long piece of stencil board, which needs to be moved much less often as you work around the room. Say that you need a 5″ (12.75 cm) border for a baseboard and that you want about ½″ (12.7 mm) clearance between the border and the baseboard. The border consists of a series of arches and sunbursts, each 6″ (15.25 cm) long, with 1″ (2.54 cm) of empty space between them.

Cut a piece of stencil board about 7″ (17.5 cm) wide and 22″ (50.8 cm) long. Measure ½″ (12.7 mm) from the bottom of the stencil board and draw a line along the length of it. The paper patterns are placed (or drawn directly) on this line so that the edge of the stencil keeps the designs ½″ (12.7 mm) away from the baseboard. Position the paper cutout (or drawing and carbon paper) on the bottom line, 1″ (25.4 mm) in from the left side of the stencil. Draw (or trace) the design on the stencil board, then move it to the right and position

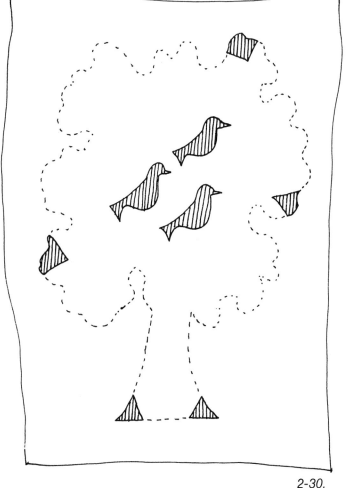

2-30.

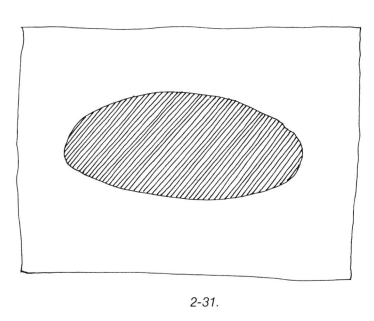

2-31.

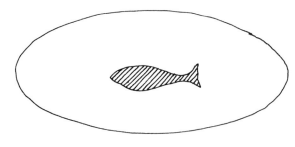

it for the next repetition. Make sure that the bottom of the design lines up with the ½" (12.7 mm) line and that the leftmost part of the second design is 1" (25.4 mm) to the right of the previous design. Draw it again, then move it to the right and position it for the third (and final) repetition. Line it up and draw it again on the stencil board. There should be 1" (25.4 mm) of space left over at the extreme right side of the stencil. Cut out the designs, the little parts first and the big parts last (cutting the big parts weakens the stencil and makes it harder for you to cut out the delicate parts). The stencil is now ready for the baseboard (fig. 2-32).

Plate 11. Single designs arranged into borders.

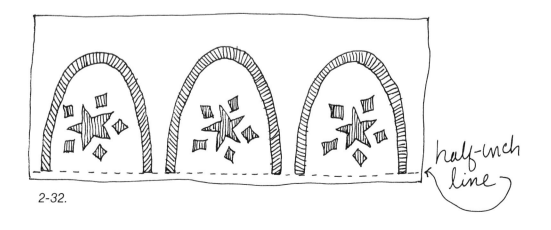

2-32.

half-inch line

The fact that the arches extended to but not beyond the drawn line made this design easy to position. Suppose that you want a design consisting only of sunbursts. If the sunburst is 4" (10.2 cm) tall and you want it to extend ½" (12.7 mm) above the baseboard, cut a strip of stencil board 5" (12.7 cm) wide to provide equal clearance at top and bottom. Draw one horizontal line through the middle of the stencil board and another through the middle of the cutout (fig. 2-33). Place the cutout on the stencil board so that the lines coincide (fig. 2-34) and you can be sure that the tracing is in the right place.

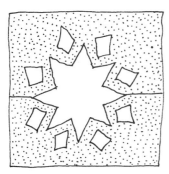

2-33.

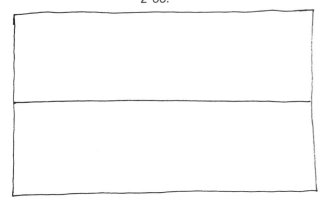

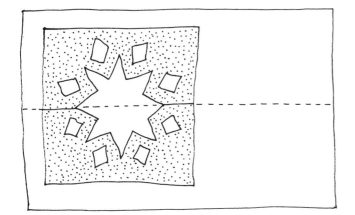

2-34.

When you're actually stenciling, you can move the border stencil along without having to measure the correct distance each time. If there's a little space between the separate designs of the border, you don't need register marks. Make sure that the space to the left of the first design on the stencil equals the spaces between the other designs. As you move the stencil to the right, position it so that its left edge just touches the last design (fig. 2-35).

If designs do not space themselves so conveniently, you can make a stencil with a cutout at the extreme left that fits over the extreme right of the previously stenciled design. In fig. 2-36 the leftmost triangle fits over the rightmost triangle in the previous design. You can move such a stencil along from left to right, creating a perfectly spaced, unbroken line of design. If the border elements are intricate, do not reproduce the entire design at the extreme left or right of the stencil: substitute a small portion of the design—a few little shapes are sufficient (fig. 2-37).

Making border stencils with more than one color isn't too hard. Make a stencil for the first color in the same way as for any border stencil. Cut another piece of stencil board in the same dimensions as the first. Place the already cut border stencil over the fresh piece of stencil board and trace all the designs, one by one, onto the new piece. This gives you the location of each separate design drawn on the stencil. Draw (or trace from a cutout) the parts to be done in a second color, being careful to place them exactly where the pencil drawings on the stencil board indicate. If you have to make a third stencil for a third color, work directly from an already cut stencil, as you did for the second color. Always trace directly from an actual stencil to accurately position the designs.

Although the instructions for making borders seem to have nothing to do with stripes, you may have guessed already that borders *are* stripes and that they are constructed in the same way. You may also have guessed from these instructions that stenciling is not the best way to reproduce designs exactly. Part of the charm of stenciling lies in the slightly soft edges of the images and in the uniqueness, however slight, of each design. Relax and enjoy making and using your stencils. Small mistakes in drawing, cutting, and measuring tend to disappear obligingly into the overall pattern, and a design that doesn't quite match the original often has virtues of its own.

make these two
spaces equal
in length

2-35.

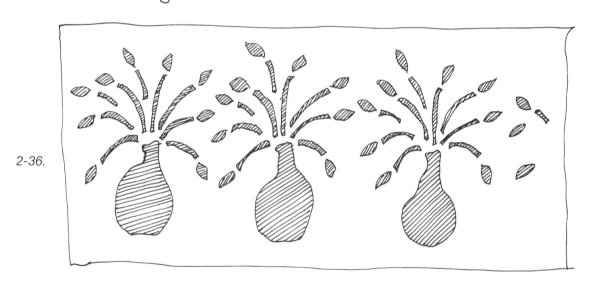

2-36.

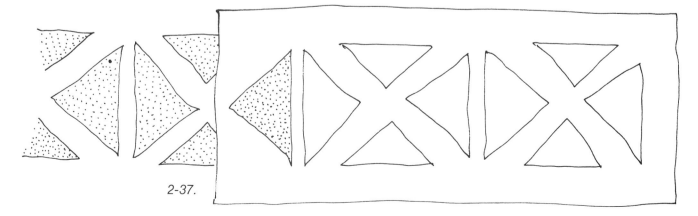

2-37.

Plate 12. Pot design.

CHAPTER 3:

INVENTING & DISCOVERING DESIGNS

A stencil design is simply the hole formed by cutting a shape in a piece of paper. The most effective stencil designs rely on shape for their appeal. This chapter describes designs for stenciling that you can find around the house, outside in the yard and street, among your hobbies and interests, and in the cultures of the world. Some of them you see every day; some you may have to research at a library or bookstore. Now is not the time to worry about the size, color, or production of a design: treat this chapter as a catalog of nice designs and how to find them.

AROUND THE HOUSE

Clothes from your own closets and drawers may contain a veritable museum of designs. Men wear ties and shirts; women wear scarves and blouses. No matter what your tastes or possessions, you're likely to find interesting geometrical, plant, and animal figures sprinkled all over your clothes. Even the simplest designs (polka dots, say) tell you something: notice the repeating pattern that they make against the background color. The colors themselves can teach you a lesson about your own taste: remember them later when you want to develop a color scheme for a stenciled room. The designs and colors of your clothing helped persuade you to buy it and wear it, and you're more likely to find an idea in your wardrobe than in so-and-so's collection of appropriate designs.

Your house contains many more such designs. Look at the wallpaper, upholstery fabric, curtains, drapes, and rugs in the various rooms. Do you prefer geometrical designs or floral prints? Make a note of designs with distinctive, graphic shapes, designs that can emerge unaltered from their surroundings.

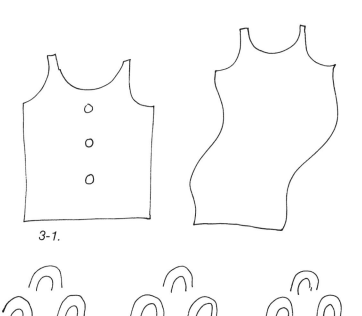

3-1.

3-2.

3-3.

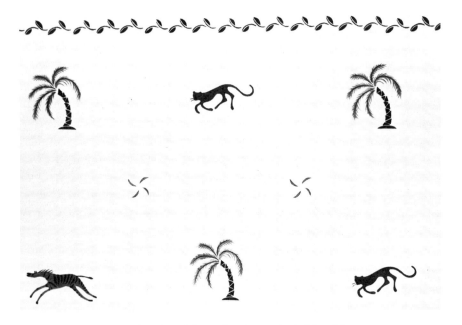

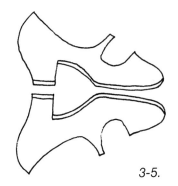

3-5.

Plate 13. The pinwheels add motion to a straight grid pattern.

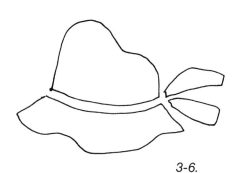

3-6.

3-7.

Plate 14. Two zebras oppose each other when the stencil is flopped over to reverse the design.

3-8.

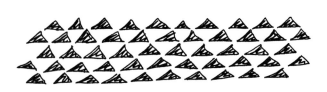

3-4.

If you like plants, look for leaf designs that you can make into twining, vinelike borders or use in clusters for allover repeating designs. Grape-ivy, Swedish-ivy, wandering-Jew, and rosary-plant leaves make good borders. Single leaves appropriate for repeating designs are those of the cut-leaf philodendron, fiddle-leaf fig, Boston fern, palm, and schefflera. For flower designs look at fuchsia, geranium, impatiens, and flowering maple. If you want to make a stencil shape of an entire plant, think about the shape of the pot, its bulk in relation to that of the plant, and the way in which the plant grows out of it. Note the sculptural shape of jade plants, succulents, cacti, and crown of thorns. Large designs of an entire plant can decorate a sun room, with some assistance from real plants, by marching along the floor in the space between baseboard and windows.

Plate 15. Columnar, stripe, and border arrangements.

3-9.

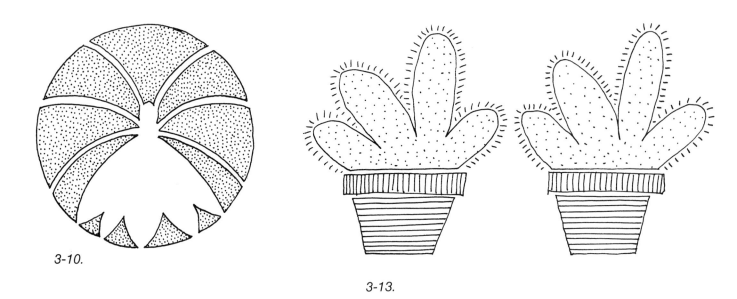

3-10.

3-13.

fuchsia

3-11.

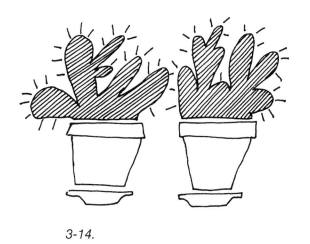

3-14.

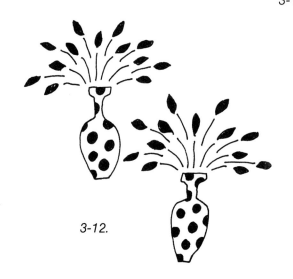

3-12.

The dining room contains unique possibilities for stencil designs. China often has a floral or geometrical border circling the rim and various floral arrangements sprinkled in the middle. The designs running up and down the handles of forks and knives could be enlarged into stenciled borders. The wraparound borders and isolated figures on cut glass are often geometrical renderings of floral motifs. Look for strong shapes as well as decorative detail. Glassware shapes include wineglasses (tulip and champagne), parfait glasses, decanters, vases, and bowls. These appealing shapes look quite formal in a Wedgwood context—plain white against a blue ground. Candlesticks and tapers can be handled in the same way. Flower arrangements, both formal and informal, contain strong, descriptive shapes and would work equally well as a simple profile or with detailed delineation of the individual flowers in several colors. All of these suggestions—glassware shapes, candlestick shapes, and bouquet shapes—would be beautiful either restricted to a wraparound border next to the ceiling or on the wall spaced at predetermined intervals on the wall.

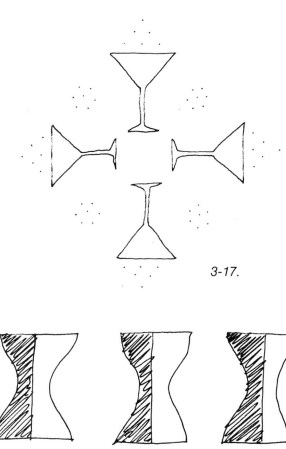

3-17.

3-18.

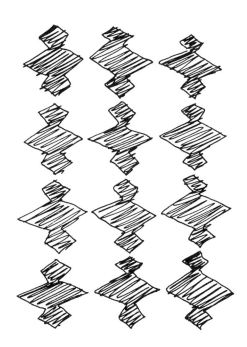

3-15.

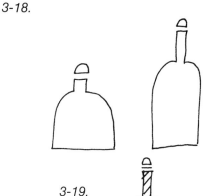

3-19.

3-16.

3-20.

Wooden chairs—ladderback, Windsor, captain's—are also shapely. A stenciled repetition of different chair shapes in silhouette would make a good border or allover design. Look for interesting carving on chairs, such as rosettes, wreaths, or cherub faces, and for needlepoint designs on the seats that might adapt to stenciling.

Most kitchens fairly teem with designs. Linoleum and shelf paper occasionally display attractive repeating designs, as do Mexican and Italian ceramic tiles. In the pantry you'll find interesting designs on can and box labels, especially if you like to buy gourmet items. A very beautiful sun design, for example, often appears on the Major Grey Chutney label. More ordinary packages display fruits, vegetables, fish, shellfish, and people (the Quaker Oats man, the Mother's Oats woman, and the SunMaid Raisin maid), many of which would look wonderful repeated on a wall. Some foods themselves are interestingly shaped: animal crackers, bugles, and related snack foods; pretzels; wheel, shell, and star pasta; windmill cookies; fruits; and vegetables all make good, strong designs. Other nifty shapes include knives, forks, spoons, spatulas, colanders, wire whisks, vegetable cookers, wire salad baskets, skillets, saucepans, wine bottles, pitchers, and coffee cups. Some of these shapes are so expressive that you would need only one simple stencil (a hole of the appropriate shape) to reproduce them.

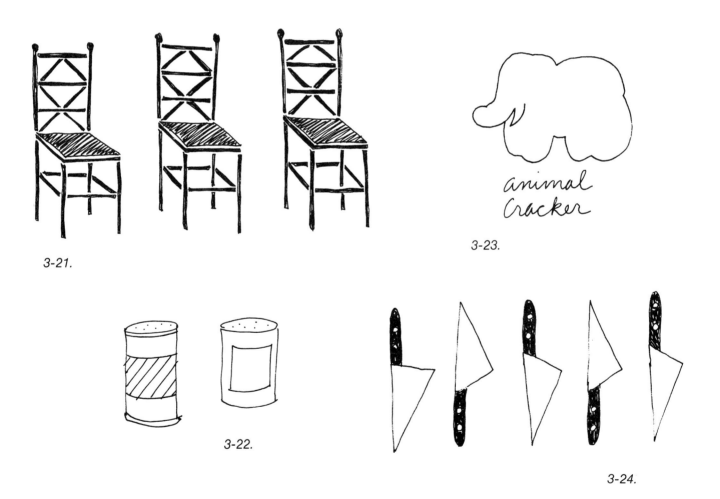

3-21.

3-23.

animal Cracker

3-22.

3-24.

34

3-25.

3-26.

3-27.

3-28.

3-29.

FROM THE YARD

In the yard you'll find plants, animals, bugs, buildings, your own vehicles, and weather. Get leaf, flower, fruit, and vegetable designs from your trees and gardens. Oak, maple, and tulip-tree leaves make good stencils by themselves or combined with their respective fruits—to create variations on the old cherry-leaves-with-dangling-cherries cliché. Try clusters of sycamore leaves with their dangling balls. You can plan an entire room around tree designs. Some stencils might show the distinctive outlines of whole trees—pines, spruces, or willows; some could represent fruit—from pears and chestnuts to catkins, maple keys, and pine cones; and, of course, you can include leaf shapes.

Some vegetables make great designs. An eggplant displays uncommon beauty, from its leaves and pale purple flower to its rambling shape and glossy, purple-black fruit. The corn plant, either in its entirety or selected parts, makes a beautiful stencil. Note the strong vertical structure, the simple opposite leaves, the decorative tassels, and the shape punctuated with pointy ears. Don't ignore the shapes of various herbs and cabbage plants or the beautiful leaves of beans.

For flowers try daisies, chrysanthemums, tulips, roses, peonies, petunias, poppies, marigolds, irises, and day lilies. In some cases, you may want to limit the design to the flower only: a side view of a petunia, say, or a head-on Japanese-style chysanthemum. In other cases you can use the whole plant for your design—irises, tulips, and day lilies, for example.

The least obvious choices for designs are the little weeds and grasses that you may never notice in your yard. Ordinary grass, with its wheatlike tassel; sorrel or sourgrass, with its delicate flower and tripartite leaves; and even dandelion plants make elegant stencil designs.

3-31.

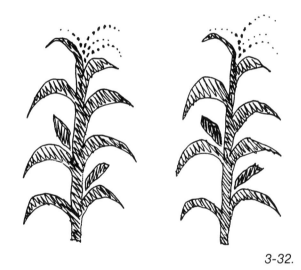

3-32.

3-30.

3-33.

36

Butterflies, moths, beetles, wasps, and yellow-jackets make good designs, as do earwigs, centipedes, aphids, ants, and hornworms, though the latter might not appeal to everyone. But keep an open mind: you can make a great stencil of a spider and web. Birds, squirrels, and even rabbits may visit your yard. A wall (or walls) of designs combining rabbits, butterflies, and tulips; wasps, apples, and spruce trees; or spiders, sourgrass, and oak leaves can bring together diverse representatives of the garden.

Plate 16. Staggered butterflies and borders.

3-34.

Now that you're outside your house, pay attention to its shape and to the shape of your car, your bicycle, and your wheelbarrow. Although these objects are not generally thought of as beautiful, they can be attractive and interesting, especially if they are stripped down to their essential structures and represented simply and honestly. Houses, with their neat, rectangular windows and doors and their peaked or gabled roof lines with chimneys and TV antennas, make splendid designs. Your house, if it is old enough, may flaunt some gingerbread—wooden carving or molding. Look for curlicues that might work in borders or as individual designs. Cars in their garages, looking like dogs in their dog houses, also have a certain appeal.

What about the weather? You can easily create symbolic representations of weather—for example, a simple, graphic depiction of lightning, a cloud, or a rainbow makes a very successful design that is useful in many different contexts. Raindrops and snowflakes, elegantly refined to their simplest outline, could be repeated polka-dot fashion all over the walls or intermixed to evoke changing conditions.

Japanese centipede

3-35.

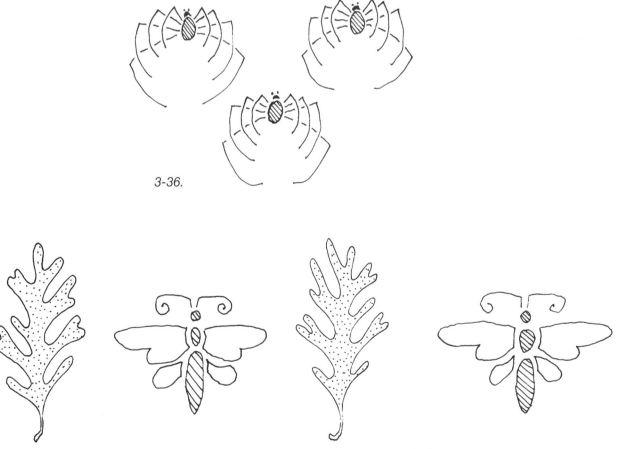

3-36.

3-37.

38

Plate 17. House, car, and cloud border.

3-38.

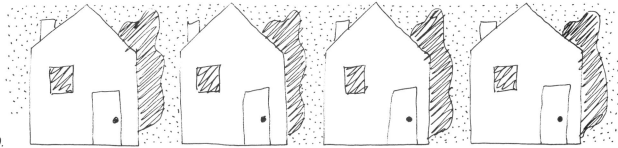

3-39.

3-40.

3-41.

3-43.

3-42.

3-44.

clouds

3-45.

IN THE NEIGHBORHOOD

Buildings and vehicles provide the most obvious design possibilities in cities and busy towns. Simple buildings reduce conveniently to Monopoly proportions and can be distinguished with added shapes. For example, you need only add a steeple to a basic house to indicate a church, or a little bell tower to the same basic shape to represent a schoolhouse. For more complicated structures such as skyscrapers, train stations, museums, department stores, or apartment houses look at as many local examples as you can to discover the qualities that make them distinctive. If you want a representative or symbolic version of a skyscraper or cathedral, say, look for photographs of the Empire State Building, Nôtre Dame de Paris, or the Lever House.

Keep an eye out for nice shapes and designs in side streets or other odd places. Man-hole covers have incongruously pretty designs. Decorative wrought-iron railings and lampposts, especially if they're old, can also provide you with designs. If you're interested in something simple and graphic, look for traffic signs and logos: sinuous or business-like arrows, road descriptions such as "slippery when wet," and bike-path designations. In the commercial section of your town don't miss the various signs displayed in shop windows. If commercial banalities fascinate you (and you aren't the only one), imagine walls covered with stylized ice-cream sundaes, high-heeled pointy-toe shoes from 1959, gas-station dinosaurs, Chiquita bananas, and dancing martini glasses. Look at billboards too: you might take a certain pleasure in stealing ideas from advertising for a change.

3-46.

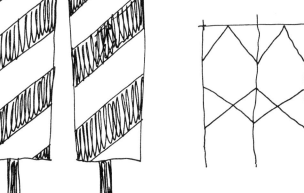

3-47.

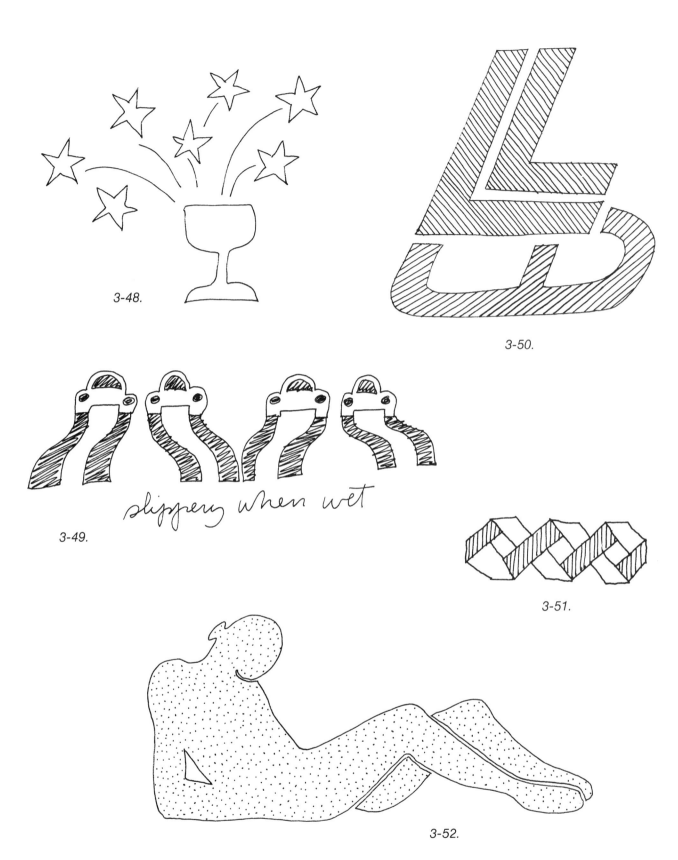

3-48.

3-50.

3-49.

slippery when wet

3-51.

3-52.

Most older cities and towns have lots of incidental sculpture standing around. Commercial buildings erected before 1930 often display carved-wood, stone, or cast-iron ornamentation. Look at the façades of old buildings, especially around the doors and windows and near the top. Many old architectural designs are in the form of borders—across the top of the building or above and below the windows, for example. Single designs (gargoyles, rosettes, and baby faces) occasionally march across the top of the building. Think about repeating some of these designs on a wall or combining them into a border. Since architectural ornamentation tends to be stiff and conventional, consider reproducing acanthus leaves and gargoyle heads in surprising colors—pink and yellow or turquoise and plum. Inside older buildings you might find pressed metal ceilings. They always have a wide border around the perimeter of the ceiling, and sometimes smaller ones that break up the ceiling into rectangular panels. Between the borders are often tile-type repeating designs that can be used either individually or in a group.

Fountains, birdbaths, and old cemetery sculpture often have appealing shapes that you can use in their entirety. If you live in a city that was fairly rich and cultured in the nineteenth century, you're certain to find giant fountains with huge Bernini-style horses thrashing around in jets of water or at least a Civil War general astride a rearing mount. A big, rich nineteenth-century graveyard such as Philadelphia's Laurel Hill or Brooklyn's Green Wood can provide you with enough angels to decorate a hundred churches, not to mention floral arrangements, sphinxes, urns, and armchairs. If you live in an exclusively modern city that is obsessed with modernity in shape and design, look at cars, trucks, buses, bicycles, trolleys, omnibuses, subways, els, trains, helicopters, airplanes, dirigibles, blimps, parachutists, unicyclists, skateboarders, and fire engines.

Plate 18. Doorway medallion, Denver Botanic Gardens.

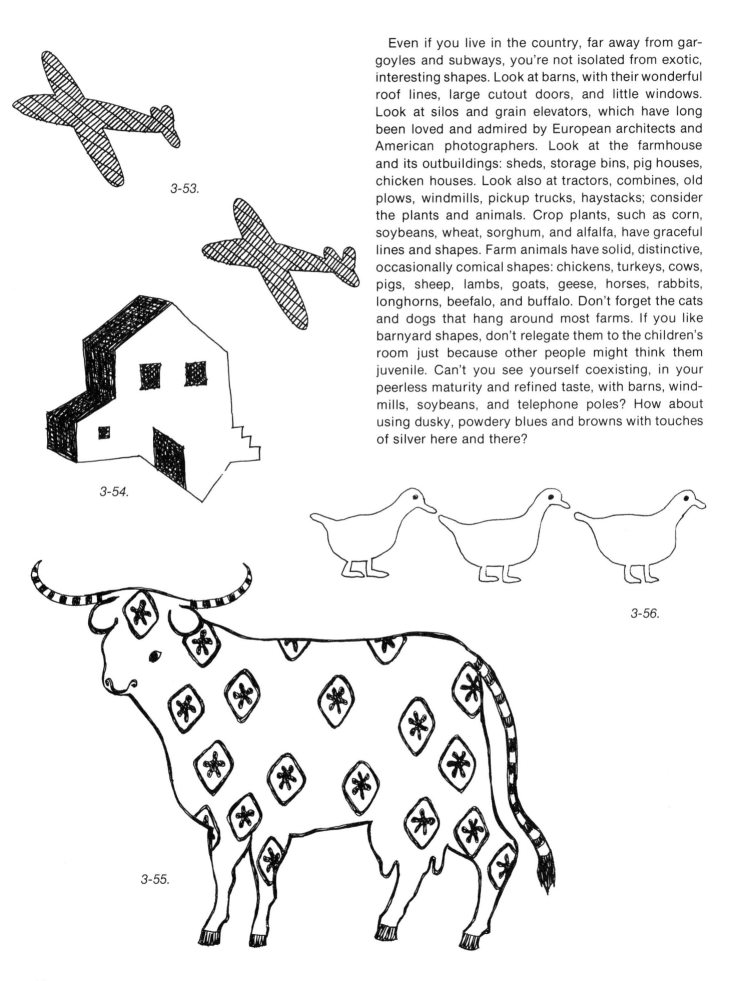

Even if you live in the country, far away from gargoyles and subways, you're not isolated from exotic, interesting shapes. Look at barns, with their wonderful roof lines, large cutout doors, and little windows. Look at silos and grain elevators, which have long been loved and admired by European architects and American photographers. Look at the farmhouse and its outbuildings: sheds, storage bins, pig houses, chicken houses. Look also at tractors, combines, old plows, windmills, pickup trucks, haystacks; consider the plants and animals. Crop plants, such as corn, soybeans, wheat, sorghum, and alfalfa, have graceful lines and shapes. Farm animals have solid, distinctive, occasionally comical shapes: chickens, turkeys, cows, pigs, sheep, lambs, goats, geese, horses, rabbits, longhorns, beefalo, and buffalo. Don't forget the cats and dogs that hang around most farms. If you like barnyard shapes, don't relegate them to the children's room just because other people might think them juvenile. Can't you see yourself coexisting, in your peerless maturity and refined taste, with barns, windmills, soybeans, and telephone poles? How about using dusky, powdery blues and browns with touches of silver here and there?

3-53.

3-54.

3-56.

3-55.

44

ON SEA AND LAND

Animals and plants with exotic shapes and gorgeous colors live in and near the ocean. You can find pictures of them in books and magazines if you have trouble remembering what they look like. Shellfish and crustaceans—snails, conches, whelks, squid, scallops, crabs, periwinkles, and lobsters—have beautiful striped and spotted shells. Whales and fish, from killer whales, with their dramatic black-and-white markings, to brilliant neon tetras in formation, make good designs. Swordfish, skates, rays, and sharks have striking forms that are simple to execute and immediately recognizable. Many-legged red starfish, seahorses, and coral all make splendid designs; there are many kinds of jellyfish, not all scary-looking. Sea anemones, kelp, other kinds of seaweed, and plankton have strong, expressive shapes, though you'll have to enlarge plankton in order to see them properly. On the shore, depending on where it is, are found pelicans, cormorants, terns, and sandpipers (only perversity prevents me from mentioning seagulls—I've been J. L. Seagulled to death). Plants come in varying shapes and sizes, many bent by prevailing winds: Monterrey cypresses, New Jersey junipers, palm trees, oceanside reeds and grasses. And don't forget the rolling waves themselves.

The zoo is crammed with strange and wonderful shapes and curious patterns: zebra stripes, leopard spots, giraffe and alligator skins. You'll certainly see lions, tigers, wallabies, and tapirs, but be sure to notice the spectacular birds—egrets, storks, cranes, parrots, flamingos, and pelicans—and snake skins. A botanical garden or book can show you plants that grow in restricted areas, plants that you're unlikely to find around the house. Look for giant tropical ferns, baobab trees, cacti, and magnificent wildflowers, such as lady's slipper, shooting star, Indian pipes, and trilliums.

Plate 19. Bedroom, Denver, Colorado.

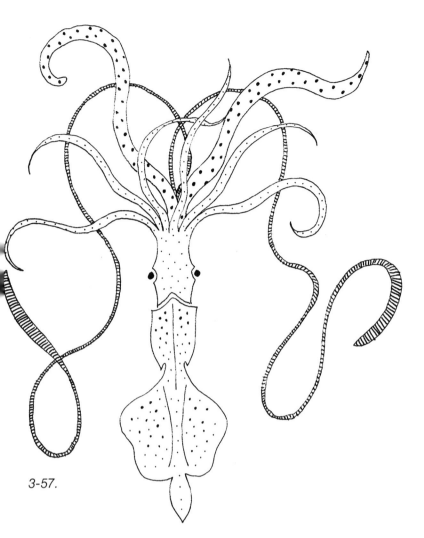

3-57.

Plate 20. Tiger pot with birds.

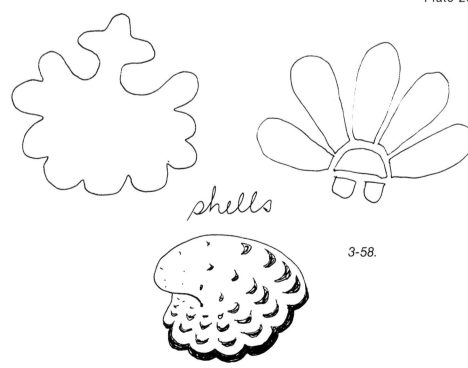

shells

3-58.

46

Plate 21. Assorted borders.

3-59.

3-60.

You can make good designs from natural wonders: volcanos, stars, comets, sand dunes, rolling hills and meadows, Mount Fuji. To make an assorted landscape (not with Mount Fuji!), overlap a group of stencils. For example, you could make a landscape entirely of dunes, all stenciled in slightly different shades of close colors and overlapping so that they recede in the distance, over which you could superimpose tiny camels, tents, and palm trees to indicate oases here and there. Man-made wonders also provide interesting shapes: sphinxes, buddhas, totem poles, mosques, pagodas, towers, oil wells, and tipis. Exotic modes of transportation that you might consider include sampan boats, paddle-wheel steamboats, luxury oceanliners, sleighs, and carriages from all periods and cultures.

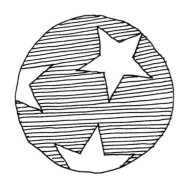

3-61.

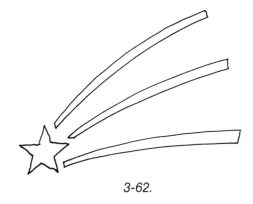

3-62.

HOBBIES AND ENTERTAINMENT

SPORTS

If you enjoy sports as either a participant or an onlooker, you're probably aware of the visual appeal inherent in sportspeople, their equipment, and their unwitting partners—antelope, trout or snow.

Fishing involves gear, fishermen, and fish; and fish always mean good shapes, nice colors, and speckles. They can be consciously exotic—sailfish, swordfish— or relatively mundane—trout, pike, catfish. Trout flies and other bait have interesting shapes and appealing colors; consider also rods, reels, and fishing boats, not to mention the bodies of fishermen twisted into tortured shapes by the straining prey.

Hunters and their dogs strike dramatic poses that translate easily into shapes for stencils; as do guns, bows, arrows, boats, decoys, and flying ducks. Alternate hunters and gear with stencils of the trees, grasses (cattails), and reeds that often accompany a hunting expedition. There is a rich selection of designs with which to compose wallsful of colorful and varied images.

Big-game hunting is fraught with great design material, much of it (as mentioned earlier) available at zoos. A border, a series of borders, or an entire wall treatment composed of animal-skin designs would be gorgeous: for example, borders of tiger and/ or zebra stripes, entire walls covered with diagonal or herringbone stripes, and walls full of leopard or giraffe spots. A series of antelope heads profiled in one color against a leopard-spotted background might border a room, or you could make several stencils, each representing a different animal head in profile, and alternate them in an allover design on every wall. You might also combine some appropriate plant life with the animals. Baobab trees, palm leaves, reeds, and vines could collaborate with various animals to evoke the jungle or the plain.

Plate 22.   Flowerpot variations.

Plate 23. Animals.

Many sports involve horses. Horse racing, gymkhanas, shows, polo, steeplechasing, and hunting are all visually appealing activities. You could easily make stencils of horses jumping and running and either alternate them in an allover pattern or restrict them to a border design. With so many thirteen-year-old girls in the world, it's not hard to imagine a bedroom decorated in this fashion. If your daughter is interested in decorating her own room, she could draw her own horses or trace them from the many magazines published for horse lovers, which characteristically show horses at their most picturesque— in mid-stride or jumping. A few different stencils of horses running with riders aboard, fences, trees, and flowering plants, all the same height, would make a great hunt panorama. Old hunt paintings frequently show all manner of flora and fauna in the garden-of-Eden style, in which everything appears to be the same size. The fact that primroses are as tall as oaks, acorns the size of riders' heads, the fox as big as the horses lends these paintings their charming air of fantasy. It also means that you can fit the different elements neatly into a border format. If horses and rider are jumping over a fence, of course, they would have to shrink down and stretch out in order to fit into the border.

Another source for sporty inspiration is television, which shows basketball, hockey, football, and soccer players leaping, charging, and thrashing around in full, colorful regalia. Since they don't stand still long enough to be drawn, you can refer to sports magazines. Look for clearly outlined athletes and either trace or draw them, simplifying the figure in the process. In many cases, as in basketball players dunking, the shape of the figure easily identifies the activity. You might add a second stencil to delineate the stripes and numbers that appear on uniforms. As usual, little sports figures—say 10″ (27 cm) high—could alternate to cover the entire wall or wrap the room in a border.

Other sports include golf, tennis, surfboarding, waterskiing, gymnastics, volleyball, track, swimming, skating, and sailing. A golfer's swing combined with the beautifully shaped trees on the golf course; a surfboarder's wave and his painted surfboard, which resembles a Masai warrior's shield; a dismount from the parallel bars; the high hurdles; and the Fosbury Flop would all make great designs. Graceful, colorful sailboats, together with seagulls and fish, are a natural subject for stenciling. Consider using the logos that appear on the sail itself—they are simple, graphic renditions of lightning, birds, and insects.

Ballet, while it is not usually regarded as a sport, may be one of your favorite pastimes, either as a participant or as an observer. You can find characteristic poses to draw in dance magazines or ask your class to hold still after hours. You can use the little figures in the same way as any design element: repeated and alternated on the wall or confined to a panoramic border. Try turning some figures upside down: you can abstract the design and lend some ambiguity to your shapes.

3-63.

3-64.

51

NONSPORTING AMUSEMENTS

Music gives pleasure to a great many people. Violins, cellos, pianos, horns of all kinds, recorders, guitars, harps, zithers, and drums have distinctive, stencilable shapes. A second stencil might delineate violin strings or the valves and holes in wind and brass instruments. If you suspect that tiny violins, pianos, and harps would appear unspeakably corny, remember that the stencils will (and should) have simple, strong, even crude outlines. They are more likely to look medieval than kitschy.

Many people collect stamps; even those who merely insist on choosing their preference at the post office might be termed collectors. There are many beautiful stamps that can provide good stencil designs. American stamps often feature native plants and animals, machinery, inventions, important people, and important events. Look for simple, descriptive outlines that you can copy easily. Stamps from other countries also depict plants, animals, and objects. The Scandinavian countries seem to specialize in extremely simple, powerful, stylized renditions. You can reproduce the stamp itself if the number, design, and words fit neatly and appealingly into their square or rectangular format. If your stamp stencils retain their outlines, you can arrange them tile fashion to cover an entire wall. You can alternate or repeat designs and colors.

People who like to cook have a built-in store of design possibilities. If you buy leeks, dill, parsley, or watercress at the grocery, take a look at their shapes—the whole leek, the parsley leaf, a few bunched leaves of watercress, dill leaves and flowers. Think about a repeating pattern composed of these forms for your kitchen or dining-room walls. For a more dynamic combination of shapes you might incorporate a whole fish (red snapper, bass, trout), a purple onion, an egg-plant, or an artichoke. Other food possibilities are desserts—many-layer cakes with their layers showing, bird's-eye views of peach tarts and strawberry cheese-cakes, lattice-topped fruit pies, cupcakes (side view), or extravagantly decorated Bavarian creams, or Jello molds.

Many cooks choose their utensils for their looks, however much they may deny it. If you pretend not to care that your spatulas are pure in shape or that your pepper mill looks like it came from the Bauhaus, you can now pay them the attention they deserve and capitalize on your good taste. Consider your gear: wire whisks, wooden forks and spoons, slotted spoons and ladles, fancy carving knives, and solid-maple ball-bearing rolling pins, though there's really no way to express the essence of maple with a stencil. Wine bottles have beautiful shapes: consider the contrasts among Burgundies, Bordeaux, Chiantis, and other more eccentric wine bottles. Wineglasses, with their characteristic shapes, provide natural supplements to the bottle theme.

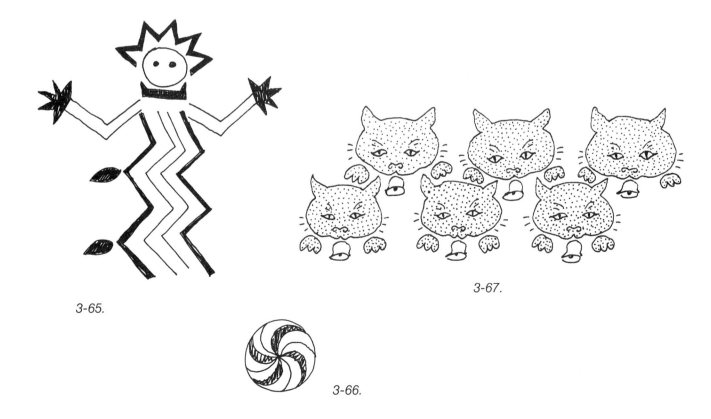

3-65.

3-66.

3-67.

The last group of personal interests concerns things that we neither do nor watch but that we like about ourselves and our life. Children's toys fit into this category, as do pets: fish, birds (and their cages), dogs (and their houses), and cats (and their dishes) would all fit nicely into the design of a room. Domestic animals are not necessarily corny subjects: avoid cute representations (big eyes, a smiling expression, big head) and ridiculous poses. Draw your animal as if he weren't your pet—don't evade his awkwardness, his mean-looking eyes, his too-thin tail. Don't invent a pretty way for him to sit or stand: try to reproduce him in a characteristic posture. Does your cat allow his tail to protrude behind him in a straight line when he sits on the floor, or does he wrap it around his feet? If you have lots of pets, do them all and rotate them regularly, polka-dot fashion, on the wall. Put yourself and your family in too. The incongruity of such a mélange constitutes part of the design's appeal.

Maybe you feel especially pleased about the region where you live or your country of origin. If your forebears were Slavic, Irish, Indian, or whatever, you probably have a wealth of tradition from which to pick designs: musical instruments, costumes, folk art, native plants and animals, architecture, sports, and landscape. If you like the area of the country in which you live, you might like to incorporate the cacti of the Southwest, the oak trees of the Midwest, the huge pine cones of California, or the maples of the East into your design plan.

3-68.

ART OF OTHER CULTURES

Most art is so universal in appeal that African masks will speak to Americans, and Japanese family-crest designs to Frenchmen. You may have a particular favorite type of folk art; you may appreciate almost any beautiful object or design, no matter what its origin. You may feel some proprietary interest in early American folk art. Museums and bookstores are full of excellent examples of beautiful designs. Weather vanes, for example, appeal to people today through their pure shapes and their often incongruous subjects: horses, people, roosters, churches, and fish all appear in stark, simple profile on early American weather vanes. Quilt designs also have wide appeal, so there are many books devoted to them. Quilt designs share, with an occasional flight of fancy, a vast vocabulary of twining vines, leafy wreaths, birds, tree shapes, repeating houses, and an amazing variety of interlocking and free-floating geometrical shapes. Since many quilts exhibit an unerring sense of composition, you might think of a quilt in terms of an entire wall and reproduce the design directly with borders and details.

The art of native Americans, always appreciated by folk-art afficionados, has recently become a national obsession. Indian designs, woven into rugs and baskets, painted on pots, and wrought in jewelry, are often abstract enough to fit neatly into almost any context. If you are not a flower-and-bird person, Indian motifs may satisfy your taste for pure design. An entire wall could be devoted to the understated, easy-to-live-with colors and calm designs of many Navaho rugs. (The so-called eye-dazzler rugs are not understated in any way, but an eye-dazzling wall or room could be spectacular!) Many rug designs can be easily adapted for borders as well.

Baskets and pots often share the same designs. If you have ever wondered why Indian pot designs are so angular, my theory is that they used to be basket designs and still conform to the strictly horizontal-vertical format imposed by the weave. Many baskets and pots display borders that run around the top of the piece: they can be lifted in their entirety and transplanted to the top of a wall. Or you can regard the whole design as a border that wraps around the piece in the same way that you plan to wrap it around the room. Many basket designs form a circular composition, best appreciated when the basket is empty and you look down into it. You might like to lift these designs as they are and transfer the disk shapes to the wall.

Plate 24. African borders.

Chinese dancer

3-69.

Plate 25. Combined early American and original designs.

Plate 26. American Indian basket design.

Totem poles make good designs, either as a whole or divided into units. Floor-to-ceiling totem poles, in very quiet, subdued colors against a dark background, can look mysterious and serene. Bits of totem poles—an animal, a bird, a humanoid face—could function as individual designs, repeating regularly in a border or covering a wall polka-dot fashion.

Some African textiles strongly resemble Indian rugs in form and color. Africans occasionally paint their homes, inside and out, and the walls around the village with similar designs. These designs need not involve a great deal of stenciling and would be fairly easy to imitate. Designs consisting of stripes and sprawling geometrical figures could be greatly reduced in size, made into stencils, and repeated in borders.

Japanese family-crest designs consist of very simple, elegant representations of plants, animals, and objects. All the designs are round. In some cases the object sits unchanged in the middle of the disk; in others it is carefully deformed into a circular outline. These designs can be repeated in borders or all over the wall—either touching at four points or slightly separated. Many of the designs can be lifted from their circular format to serve in any other context. They don't have to be treated as circles. Check the motifs on Japanese lanterns and fans as well.

If you live in a very large city—New York, Chicago, Los Angeles—you can probably buy sheets of stenciled paper from a Japanese-import store. Ordinary import stores often sell objects covered with this paper—pencil holders, address books, small all-purpose boxes. Since the designs are actual stencils, they are often easy to reproduce. The uniform, unbroken fields of design—no borders—are closer approximations of wallpaper than most stencils. Since the design elements are quite tiny, I would recommend enlarging them considerably: the larger the design, the easier it is to see and the less time it takes to cover a wall.

Plate 27. Bedroom, Eldorado Springs, Colorado.

3-70.

Plates 28, 29, and 30. Details of bedroom, Japanese crest designs.

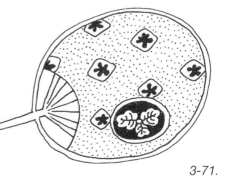

3-71.

REFERENCE BOOKS

If you get very involved in finding and inventing designs, you might decide to buy some books. Before you run off to the bookstore, however, consider the books that you can find at the library. Books on ancient cultures—Egyptian, Inca, Mayan, and Olmec, for example—generally include many examples of designs on clothing, documents, jewelry, sculpture, and architecture. Nature books often have bright, colorful plates of ocean and inland plants and animals. Books on modern cultures (American Indian, African, Eskimo, and South Pacific) show examples of folk art as part of their coverage. There are many books specifically about folk art, which feature detailed examples of American, Mexican, Japanese, European, Scandinavian, African, and American Indian decoration.

If you're looking for design sources, go to a bookstore with a generous selection of art and design books. Reprints of texts used by designers in the nineteenth and early twentieth centuries are available, such as W. and G. Audsley's *Designs and Patterns From Historic Ornament*, originally published in 1882. The designs are unquestionably authentic, informatively categorized according to use and form, and shown in both borders and allover patterns, which makes this a good reference for a beginning designer. Other interesting reprints include books on Japanese and Chinese stencil, lattice, and flower designs; Indian basket weaving; art-nouveau and art-deco designs; and designs of many other periods, including, amusing as it may seem, the 1950s. Among current books on design are some that deal specifically with stenciling as an art form. Collections of Victorian and early American stencils are available, many of which contain full-scale designs from actual stencils that can be cut out and used directly. Other crafts can be used as sources for stencil designs, among them American furniture and metalware painting, patchwork quilts, African designs, and Victorian cemetery art (good for angels).

Many magazines contain lovely photographs of a variety of subjects, many suitable for stencil designs. *National Geographics*, old (available at used-book stores and libraries) or new, almost always devote some space to exotic plants and animals, peculiar topography, picturesque people, and folk art. *Ranger Rick* is the eight-year-old's *Geographic:* it's full of fantastic photographs of animals and plants (but no picturesque people or folk art!). House-and-home magazines can give you ideas for colors, themes, and motifs via ads for and photographs of wallpaper, upholstery and drapery fabrics, tiles, and even the knickknacks that they insist on scattering over every level surface. Comic books and children's picture books make good reference texts for a playroom or a child's bedroom. They can also help you out in surprisingly formal settings, as they often contain stylized renderings of plants, animals, people, and objects in sophisticated colors.

Plate 31. Japanese stenciled cloth.

Plate 32. Early American designs.

ADAPTING DESIGNS FOR STENCILING

Look for strong shapes. A simple stencil is merely a hole cut in a piece of heavy paper: make sure that it has an interesting, recognizable (or pleasantly ambiguous) outline. A wine bottle, horse, palm tree, basketball player, or cactus is a clear shape that can be recognized without additional clues from detail or color. A more complicated stencil has more than one hole. Make sure that the series of holes makes sense as a unit and forms a recognizable object. A lobster, for example, might consist of one hole indicating the body, another hole for the tail, and more holes for the claws and feelers. These holes are drawn and cut into the stencil so that together they depict a lobster. An oil-well rig indicated by only one hole would look like a tall, truncated triangle—neither revealing nor especially attractive. A series of holes cut in the stencil would indicate the structure more expressively—narrow slitlike holes could delineate the recognizable horizontal and vertical struts and beams that form the derrick.

Look for designs that don't depend on shading. A complicated shaded photograph of a group of trees, for example, would not make a good stencil design. Look instead for the outline—clean, distinctive, and whole—of a single tree and use it with one or two others if you want a group of trees. If shading is necessary to make a design comprehensible, you probably won't be able to use the design—you will at least have to change its structure. A stencil of an antelope's head, for example, cannot define the distance between the nose and eyes as regarded head-on. Either show the head in profile or use flat colors and markings to delineate the straight-on face.

Look for a minimal number of colors: the fewer the colors, the fewer the stencils that you have to make. Most designs stand out more clearly and graphically in only two or three colors. Too many colors can obscure the purity of the shape.

Look for a design that doesn't depend on crowded, intersecting lines. Don't try to reproduce a scene from an etching or the many branches of a tree. Reduce the tree to a leafy shape with a trunk or to a few branches with two or three leaves and a fruit on each. Arrange the subjects so that their lines don't cross each other. To make a stencil of a vine, for example, arrange the stems and leaves so that they neither touch nor cross. Such a design resembles those on quilts, in which the central stem moves along in a straight or serpentine fashion but the leaf stems project outward in an orderly way, one every 2" (5 cm) or so, and the leaves sit primly at the ends of the leaf stems.

If your design depends upon a line, make it as simple as possible. If you want a blue outline of a bear against a white background, for example, make the outline fairly heavy and very simple and leave spaces here and there. These spaces, or ties, will keep the center of the stencil from falling out so that you end up with a white bear on a white wall with a blue outline instead of a solid blue bear on a white wall.

Include distinguishing features in a design. If you want to stencil tomatoes, for example, their shape and color should not be the only distinguishing characteristics. Include some leaves and a bit of vine and/or stem in the stencil so that they are not mistaken for apples! Some objects have shapes in common but can be distinguished from each other by their surface design. A zebra and a horse, for example, are similar in shape. If you want a zebra, make a separate stencil for the stripes and apply it on top of the already stenciled shape so that there can be no mistaking your intention.

The most important consideration is to keep your imagination open to designs from all possible sources and to feel free to mix them up in any way at all. See how they feel together—an oil well, a cantaloupe slice, and a scallop shell, for example. Isn't there something appealing about such juxtapositions? Yes, indeed there is.

Plate 33. Combined authentic, original Victorian designs.

Plate 34. Bedroom, Boulder, Colorado.

CHAPTER 4:

PLANNING A ROOM

Stenciling is simple to plan and execute, flexible, and personal. You can put any design anywhere with little to fear from technical problems or cost. Distinctive architectural features that make wallpapering awkward or impossible—odd angles, sloping walls, doors—provide ideal surfaces for stenciled designs; rooms with ordinary proportions, on the other hand, can be enlivened and visually reshaped with carefully coordinated stenciled patterns. Before you begin to worry that the very number of possibilities will make it impossible for you to decide what to do, consider the conceptual simplicity of stenciling: all stenciled rooms are composed of nothing more than borders and field designs.

BORDERS

Borders frame walls, doors, and windows, calling attention to their rectangular format. On a wall the effect imitates an oriental rug or bedspread, the borders of which prepare the eye to perceive a field design on the inside (fig. 4-1). Such a border is usually from 4″ to 12″ (10.2 to 31 cm) wide. The borders that frame doors and windows tend to be narrower—from 2″ to 4″ (5.1 to 10.2 cm) wide—and in most rooms they should match (fig. 4-2). Borders emphasize the geometrical relationships among windows, doors, and walls and the pleasing compositions that they create in a room.

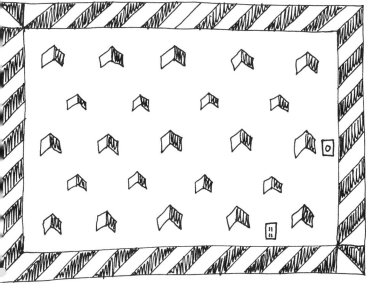

4-1.

4-2.

Plate 35. Guest room, Boulder, Colorado.

Other borders wrap horizontally around a room. They follow the line of the ceiling, the baseboard, or horizontal molding such as dado and chair rails. Since the four walls break up a room into four distinct planes, horizontal borders can integrate it by wrapping it in a continuous, all-encompassing band of design. The most prominent place for such a border is at the top of the wall, where neither furniture nor artwork interferes with the view. The border can be rich in color and design and can range, depending on the height of the ceiling, from 10″ to 24″ (26 to 62 cm) in height. A baseboard border often repeats the top-of-the-wall design (fig. 4-3) and visually pulls together the various pieces of furniture arranged around the room's perimeter.

A dado is a strip of molding that encircles a room at hip or waist level. Wainscoting may extend from it to the floor. A similar molding that runs around the room at a level closer to the ceiling is called a chair or picture rail—grandmothers balance commemorative plates on it. Borders that accompany dado and chair-rail moldings emphasize their tendency to pull a room together, drawing walls around an arrangement of furniture (dining table and chairs, for example) and creating a feeling of intimacy (fig. 4-4). Dado borders often run around windows and doors as well (fig. 4-5). Since chair rails are near the ceiling, they usually demand wide, prominent borders. You may decide to fit a very large border into the space between the chair rail and the ceiling, filling 10″ to 18″ (26 to 46 cm) with solid design (fig. 4-6).

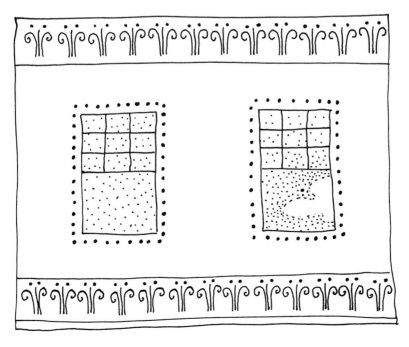

4-3.

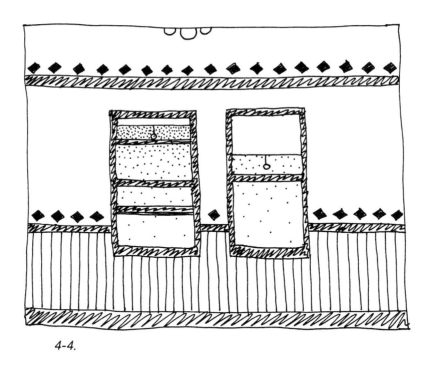

4-4.

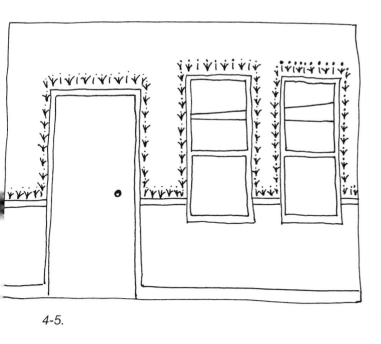

4-5.

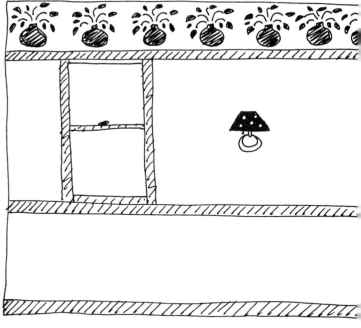

4-6.

FIELD DESIGNS

Once you have defined the contours of the room with borders, consider the kind of field design you want, if any. Field designs integrate the various objects and artwork that you hang on a wall, pulling them together into one composition. Field designs can be busy or quiet, depending on the room's need or tolerance for visual stimulation. The basic format for allover patterns is the grid.

Imagine that your walls are covered with a penciled 12″ (31 cm) grid—the vertical and horizontal lines are 12″ apart, and the squares that they form are 12″ square. In the exact center of each square is a tulip-tree leaf. The pattern that emerges when the grid is erased is the simplest grid pattern that you can design (fig. 4-7). You can complicate it by adding more designs—a dragonfly and a snail, for example—and using them in various rotations (fig. 4-8). By enlarging or shrinking the grid and/or the

designs you can change the character of the patterns a great deal. They can look lively and informal or quiet and calm (fig. 4-9).

You can make staggered grid patterns with the same stencils and a slightly different imaginary grid—say, with 6″ (15.2 cm) squares. Taking your tulip-tree-leaf stencil to the first vertical column of squares, put a design in the middle of the top square. Skip the next square and put the design in the third. Put leaves in every other square until you reach the floor. At the second column of squares leave the top square empty and begin your every-other-square alternation in the second square. At the third column revert to the original scheme, putting a leaf in the top square and in every other square on down (fig. 4-10). The staggered grid is conceptually similar to the plain grid but much livelier: the leaves tend to "dance" on the wall. Add the dragonfly and snail if you want even more excitement and try out various rotations (fig. 4-11).

Plate 36. Bedroom, Yorkville, Illinois.

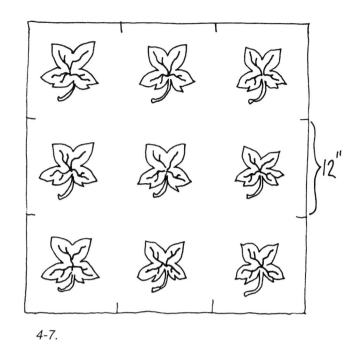

4-7.

4-8.

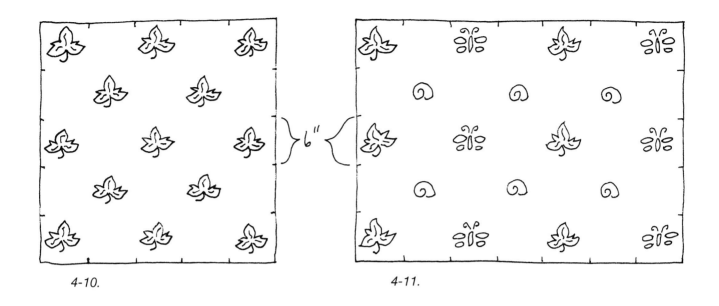

4-10.   6"   4-11.

Plate 37. Bedroom, Boulder, Colorado.

Trellis designs are created by stenciling the grids themselves onto the walls in the form of stripes. If you turn the trellis grid 45 degrees, diamond-shaped rather than square panes are formed. Treat the centers of the panes with single or rotated designs (fig. 4-12). You can try various stripe arrangements using different grids as the structural basis. Imagine a grid on the wall with vertical lines 2′ (62 cm) apart and horizontal lines 1′ (31 cm) apart. At the intersections of the lines are tulip-tree leaves. If the tops and bottoms of the leaves are separated by a few inches of space, they form columns (fig. 4-13); if they touch, they form stripes (fig. 4-14). With different grids the spacing of the stripes changes (fig. 4-15). Stripes can decorate a wall by themselves, or you can rotate various designs between them to form new compositions (fig. 4-16).

Any allover pattern changes radically if the designs are enlarged until they touch in four directions and form a continuous network (fig. 4-17). The result resembles wallpaper and is in fact the basis for many wallpaper designs. Like wallpaper, these designs *may* look best without framing borders. Stenciling alone allows you the choice, however, and the opportunity to use the same design to produce discreet, elegantly spaced, formal patterns or exuberantly colorful, crowded images. Such possibilities make stenciling the flexible art form that it is.

Stenciling is flexible in other ways. It works in any room, no matter how large, small, formal, informal, dark, or light. It can improve a room by accentuating its good features and by disguising its flaws. It can create an entirely new mood or underscore one that already exists. You can apply stenciling to virtually any surface—rough walls, boxed-in ducting and conduits, strangely shaped and angled architectural features (stairs, bay windows, upstairs nooks and crannies). You can cover your whole house, inside and out, or you can limit your designs to a pot of flowers over the front door. Though all rooms are as different and varied as people's tastes, there are a number of guidelines to follow in planning stenciled designs.

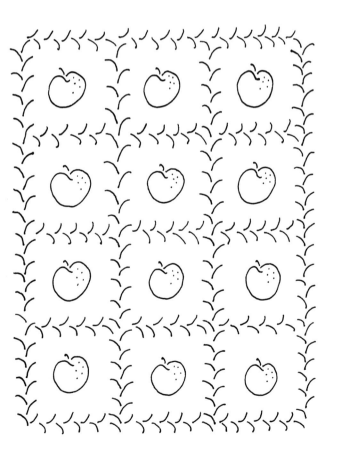

4-12.

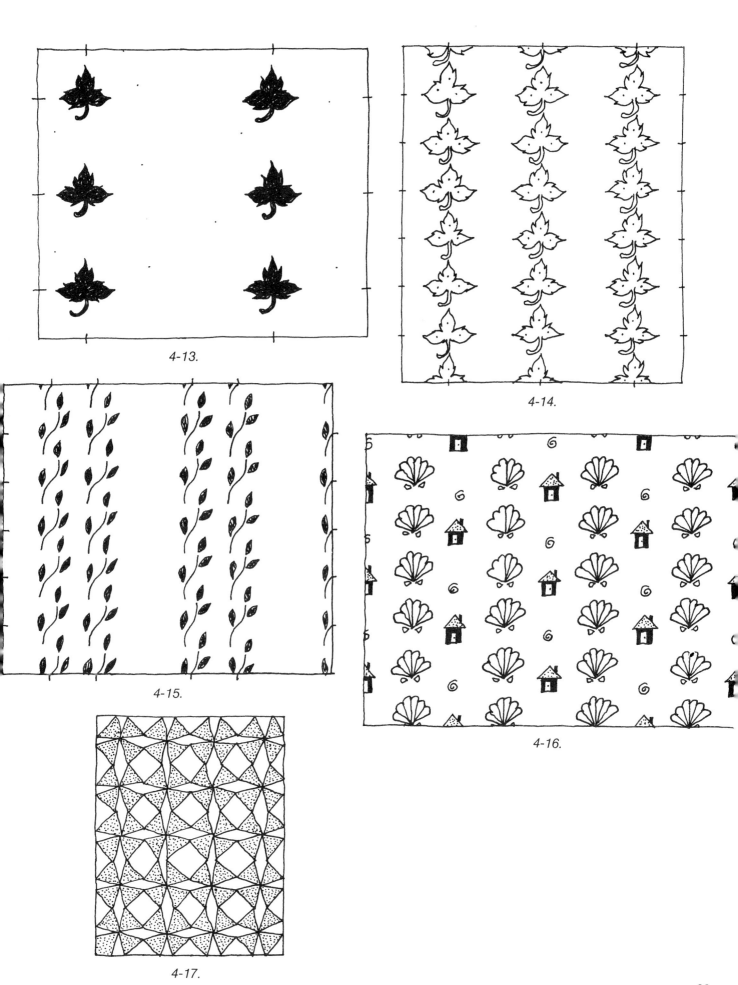

4-13.

4-14.

4-15.

4-16.

4-17.

LARGE ROOMS

Large rooms, with their many furnishings and abundant space, demand that you unify and tie together the various elements. You want coherence and order while ensuring at the same time that the walls don't entirely dominate the space. Unite the four walls of the room with a wraparound border at the top and another at the baseboard. Find a border for the windows and doors with the same (or similar) colors and shapes and use it everywhere.

An allover design can unify the various objects and paintings that you display on the walls. To prevent the walls from becoming unpleasantly overbearing, you might keep the field designs rather small—maybe 4″ (10.2 cm) in diameter—and widely spaced—perhaps 18″ (46 cm) apart. Keep the designs calm and predictable by using a regularly spaced or staggered grid pattern that conforms to fairly precise measuring.

SMALL ROOMS

Small rooms offer more design freedom than you may suspect. The very smallness prevents overpopulation: you can fit just so many designs into a little space. Most small rooms don't have much furniture to compete with the walls (guest rooms have a bed, a chair, a dresser) and no drapes or fancy lighting fixtures. And most small rooms—sewing room, study, bedroom—are not public places. If you have a taste for high-powered visual stimulation, you can enjoy it without offending anyone else. Small rooms that *are* public are often places that one passes through quickly: hallways, foyers, guest bathrooms, for example. You can lavish design and color on them—no one will be there long enough to get tired of them. Small rooms should be bright spots in the house, and they should have personalities of their own.

Plate 38. Bedroom, Boulder, Colorado.

Plate 39. Powder room, Vail, Colorado.

Plate 40. Dining room, Boulder, Colorado.

Use bright, crowded designs if you want to. The effect will be informal, and you can emphasize the informality with transparent colors; open, airy designs; and slightly imprecise measuring. If the ceilings are low, as they're apt to be, avoid ponderous wraparound borders. Pick a narrow, open, light border design—perhaps to match that used around the windows and doors. Choose bright, lively prints for curtains and bedspreads. The colors don't have to match, and the designs may be unrelated. Just pick something with spirit—subtle patterns and colors get lost in a colorful room.

FORMAL AND INFORMAL ROOMS

Formal rooms, like very large rooms, abhor chaos. Most revolve around a carefully chosen, closely related collection of furniture and accessories, often belonging to a specific period. Choose colors and designs that relate directly to them. Tie the room together with wraparound borders and use a regularly repeating pattern of small designs for the field. Avoid crowding the designs and make your measurements and placement as precise as possible.

There is a style of formality, however, that celebrates the richness of the world by combining chintz, chinoiserie, and exotica with period furniture. Designs for such a room should be fairly large (they have a lot to compete with), colorful, and very lush. Try richly colored flowers, birds, and animals.

Informal rooms should be handled like small rooms or ordinary large ones. Generally speaking, you can do almost anything within the limitations imposed by the room's size.

CAPITALIZING ON GOOD POINTS

All rooms have their points, and stenciling can help you enhance them. In some cases these points consist of nothing more than an attractive placement of windows or the restful rectangles of the walls. Borders outlining these features bring them to the viewer's attention, encouraging him to ignore other less attractive features.

Most rooms with fireplaces have a blank space over the mantelpiece—the traditional site for the best painting or for special stenciled decoration. The old-fashioned approach to the overmantel was to outline the space with borders and to arrange stencils in a symmetrical pattern that filled up the field (fig. 4-18). While there's no reason for you to use the same designs, you can borrow the concept and put especially large, graphic, and colorful images in the overmantel space.

Some rooms have strange and interesting shapes built into them in the form of dormers, gables, and sloping walls. Borders outlining their angles and planes emphasize the curious compositions produced by eccentric walls and windows. You'll have a lot of fun (I'm not being ironic) fitting allover designs into the strangely shaped fields delineated by the borders. Design your stenciling to accentuate the mood of the room: for example, you might want to make a sloping wall over a bed into a snug, intimate nook by stenciling behind the bed and extending the designs up to and across the ceiling. The canopy effect can be further exaggerated if you paint the wall and ceiling a color that contrasts with the rest of the room.

Extralarge windows and a sunny exposure provide some rooms with especially beautiful light. Intensify the light by painting the walls white or a light pastel color. Choose fairly transparent colors for the stenciling—clear reds, yellows, oranges, and greens. The designs should be open and airy, the borders delicate. The light and the designs will enhance each other, particularly in the afternoon when the sun is at its warmest and most golden.

In planning any room look for ways to decorate unusual doorways (arches, fancy molding), bay windows, and interesting curves and angles in the walls themselves—in short, anything that makes your room more complicated than the essential box. If you treat these features as if they were worth honoring, they'll add a great deal of distinction to the room.

IMPROVING AWKWARD FEATURES

Many rooms, especially modern ones, include strange vertical or horizontal (hung from the ceiling) protrusions—boxed-in heating ducts, structural members, or conduits. Borders that outline the various planes can integrate a protrusion into the rest of the room. You can either use the same field design that you've used everywhere else or put entirely new designs on the boxed-in surface, making a kind of minigallery (fig. 4-19).

Suppose that the very shape of the room is awkward—say, a long, narrow living room that makes you feel as if you're on a train. Besides painting the long walls a recessive color and the short ones a more aggressive, warmer color you can play some stenciling tricks to make the walls behave the way you want them to. If you decide to use an allover pattern in the room, you can change the colors, spac-

Plate 41. Bedroom, Boulder, Colorado.

Plate 42. Turn-of-the-century border, Denver, Colorado.

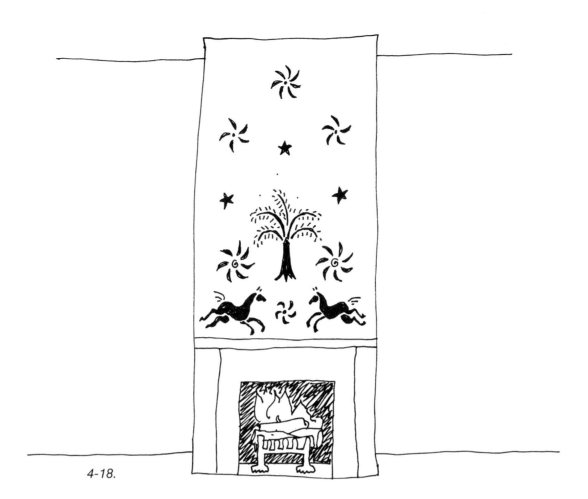

4-18.

4-19.

ing, and size of the designs to bring walls closer or make them keep their distance. Warm colors, close spacing, and large designs put a wall in your lap (maybe this intimacy is just what you crave); cool, recessive colors and small, far-apart designs keep them at bay. You can use just one of these tricks or all of them very subtly—the changes don't need to be at all drastic.

The rooms in an old house have generally been patched over the years and show it. In some cases the walls are uneven enough to make wallpapering a difficult task. Colorful and lively stenciled designs cause such imperfections to disappear: the busier the designs, the more impenetrable the disguise. Avoid putting very formal designs on such a surface: the same quality that demands precise spacing dictates surface evenness.

Most walls are interrupted by doors, windows, stairs, fireplaces, or molding. Occasionally a wall traverses a room unrelieved by any kind of interruption, and the effect can be unbearable. Stenciling allows you to break down walls in several different ways. One solution imitates paneled molding—using a narrow border design, draw a series of rectangles on the long wall. In the fields created by the borders you can plan allover patterns (fig. 4-20). Horizontal molding—chair rails and dados—can also destroy the solidity of an unbearably large, blank wall. If you don't have any, you can paint it in—on all the walls. Run borders along your painted-in molding: fit a broad border between the "chair rail" and the ceiling, for example, or let a lacy border follow the "dado" around the room. A heavy, densely spaced field design located below the dado imitates wainscoting. Above the dado you can stencil in an airier, more spacious pattern.

Some rooms have doors and windows in every wall—no problem there—but all the windows may be different sizes, and the doors different heights. Strong borders around the windows and doors can do a lot to unify them and make the room look less chaotic. If the doors and windows are strangely spaced or unpleasantly asymmetrical, you can tie them together with painted-in chair-rail and dado molding.

Plate 43. Model room, May D & F, Denver, Colorado.

74

CREATING A MOOD

One of the most exciting things that you can do to a room is to use designs and colors to create an entirely new atmosphere, a different mood. Because it's difficult to instill a feeling of romanticism or mystery in a white wall, begin with the right background colors. The size, type, and function of the room and the kind of light that it receives can help you choose the color.

Your design choice is limitless: anything from dancing martini glasses in yellow and pink against a deep green background to fleurs-de-lis in pale blue against cream. International designs or folk-art motifs lend exoticism to a room: get designs from the library or bookstore or invent your own adaptations. If you want to plan a room around a central influence—Mexico, Japan, African sculpture, or big-game hunting—stenciling is probably the easiest way to achieve an integrated look.

Plate 44. *Arch congruence*, Denver Botanic Gardens.

4-20.

STENCILING WHERE WALLPAPER FEARS TO TREAD

In Chapter 6 I discuss stenciling on doors, window shades, ceilings, floors, and miscellaneous fixtures such as floorcloths and bathtubs. You should, however, consider these possibilities while you're planning a room. You should also decide whether or not to stencil on your staircase, on the kitchen cabinets, or inside the corner cupboard.

People nowadays tend to prefer unpainted stairs, but this wasn't always true, as those of you with white stairs know. If you can stand the idea of painting them again, try a dark, rich color. You can stencil small designs on the banister, spindles, and the sloping zigzag that accompanies the treads and risers (fig. 4-21). Borders stenciled on the walls can slope with the stairs (fig. 4-22). If the treads and risers are uncarpeted, you can center one or several designs on each or run borders up the sides (fig. 4-23).

You can stencil on unpainted woodwork without much difficulty. Before you put designs on the insides or outsides of cabinets and cupboards, remove the gloss or varnish with liquid sandpaper. Special one-of-a-kind designs work well, as do narrow borders. Keep the designs fairly delicate and uncrowded.

4-22.

4-23.

4-21.

PLANNING IN ADVANCE

Because stenciling should reflect your taste accurately and because it allows you to change and adjust designs until they're perfect, it requires thoughtful planning. Two aids in planning are graph paper (four squares to the inch) and crescent board.

Let one square equal 6" (15.2 cm) and draw one wall on each piece of graph paper. Xerox the four pieces so that you have at least five copies of each to play with. Using the grid of the squares as a guide, plot border and field designs for each wall. In most cases you'll want to use the same layout everywhere, but eccentric architectural features may require you to adjust some of the designs so that they fit properly. The graph paper also allows you to try alternative patterns: if you find that vertical stripes look too rigid, you can draw in a staggered grid instead. You can change the placement and size of the designs; you can see how they look with and without borders.

Do your advance planning of colors on 30"-×-40" (78-×-100 cm) crescent board. Most art-supply stores carry a wide range of colors, and you can often find a color that nearly matches your walls. If not, buy a plain sheet and paint it the correct background color with the same latex that you used in the room. Cut out the stencils and try them out in advance on the crescent board. Make sure that the colors look nice together, that you like the way the designs work, and that you're pleased with the spacing. You can make the changes you want by painting over the wrong colors through the stencil or by erasing the entire design with a coat of latex paint and starting over. Whatever adjustments you have to make, it's easier to make them on crescent board. And a beautiful crescent board will give you the confidence that you need to thoroughly enjoy stenciling on the wall—as you should.

Plate 45. Stenciled crescent board.

Plate 46. Drawing room, Mark Twain Memorial, Hartford, Connecticut.

CHAPTER 5:

WALL STENCILING

Anyone who can stencil on paper can stencil on a wall. Thoughtful preparation of walls and materials and knowledge of stenciling techniques make the job easy and fun. This chapter describes the materials to buy at the art-supply store, explains how to fit stencils in corners of rooms and around door and window moldings, and how to space allover patterns without elaborate measuring.

In most cases you have to paint the walls before stenciling, if only to give yourself the cleanest possible surface to start with. Paint right over ordinary walls—stucco peaks have to reach Himalayan proportions before they need preliminary smoothing. If you must sand, use an electric sander and very coarse paper: it will take an hour at most. Paint with latex or oil-based paint, preferably flat or satin. You *can* stencil on a glossy surface, but it's tricky and the results will not be as durable as they should—no paint can effectively penetrate a glossy surface. You can always provide gloss later with varnish. Paint in any bands of color for borders, wainscoting, dado, and/or chair-rail molding at the same time. Use masking tape to establish straight lines. You can also establish curved lines if you put a series of cuts on the *outside* of the tape as it follows the curve.

SUPPLIES

I usually use acrylic paint for stenciling, because it is fast-drying, water-soluble, and relatively washable. Many brands are available and I haven't tried them all, but I like Liquitex because of its smooth texture. Most projects require very little paint, so you can buy your colors in 2-ounce (59 ml) tubes. Buy plenty of white: it's a very useful (and inexpensive) color. You can get by with fewer colors, but my standard selection consists of: cadmium red medium, phthalocyanine and Hooker's green, ultramarine blue, dioxazine purple, cadmium yellow, mars black, and titanium white.

There is no brown on the list because you can make gorgeous browns with red and black or with green and red. You can, in fact, make virtually any color in the world with the above selection except bubblegum pink (if you're bent on it, get alizarin crimson). If you have a choice between dark and light versions of a color—cadmium red medium or cadmium red light, for example—pick the dark version. You can always lighten a dark color with white or water, but darkening muddies a light color. And, of course, if you find any paints that are closer to your color scheme than the ones on my list, get them and save yourself some mixing.

Since you probably won't use the paints right from the tube (tube colors are usually too bright, too dark, or too transparent), get some containers for mixing and storing colors. The best that I know of are ricotta-cheese containers—they're like free Tupperware. You can also use baby-food jars, yogurt containers, or large spice jars. In mixing a color try to fill half a ricotta container (a little less than a cup). This is usually too much paint, but it's obviously better to have too much than too little, and it largely consists of water in any event.

To make light blue, for example, put a large squeeze of blue into the container with a liberal dollop of white. Add a dash of water—enough to make the mixture stirable—and stir with a stick or brush. Add more water until the texture approaches that of pea soup or vichyssoise and adjust the color by adding blue or white as needed. The more that you add to a color, the more opaque it becomes, and the better your chances of covering in one coat. I often add white to red, yellow, blue, and green just to decrease their natural transparency. If you want a transparent color, don't add white to lighten it—add water. The paint will be a little runny, so you'll have to use an almost-dry brush to keep it from dripping, which further increases the transparency of the color. To complicate or dull colors slightly (they can be awfully brash), add tiny bits of red to green, green to red, red and yellow to blue, green and red to yellow. Adding black makes colors grayer; adding white makes fascinating, ambiguous pastels.

You can save paint by not mixing every color in advance. If you're going to use two greens, for example, a light and a dark, mix the dark one first. When you're finished stenciling with it, put some aside for an emergency—a little place that you forgot to do or a smudge that mysteriously appears on a dark green leaf. Use the remainder as a base for the light green: add yellow, white, or whatever you need plus the appropriate amount of water.

Everyone runs out of a color occasionally—it's not a tragedy. Remix it as best you can remember without worrying about the proportions. When you stir the color, you can tell by looking at it if it needs any additions. Adjust it until it looks fairly close and make it slightly lighter than the color that you're matching, since acrylic darkens as it dries. Most stencil designs are separated by spaces, if only the products of ties, so the new color needn't match the original perfectly. Do rug-knotting nomads worry when they run out of a dye lot? Don't you worry either.

Plate 47. Bedroom, Yorkville, Illinois.

If you love the idea of 10′ totem poles, you should know that you can also stencil with latex paint. If you want to cover very large areas with solid colors, the expense of acrylic can be a problem. You can get just about any latex color ready-mixed (though paint stores vary widely in their selections). It's usually the right consistency for stenciling, but you can thin it with water if necessary.

You can buy brushes for acrylics at any art-supply store. They have flattened bristles that are cut straight off at the end. The soft, dark-bristled brushes work well; sable brushes work best of all and are certainly the most durable, but they are expensive. Get one brush about ¾″ (19mm) wide and another about ½″ (12.7 mm) wide. There are special brushes made just for stenciling—you stipple the colors on—but I like conventional brushes best, and they work better on a rough surface. If you like stippling brushes, however, by all means use them.

Buy masking tape to tape stencils to the wall and perform other miracles. A few large sheets of a stiff paper such as bristol board enables you to enlarge your stencils so that they space themselves. Other items that you need are: water in a can or jar, a small cloth or paper towel, scissors, pencil, and tapemeasure. You should already have an X-acto knife.

STENCILING TECHNIQUES

Wall stenciling differs little from stenciling on paper, but it's infinitely more exciting. After days of preparation—making the stencils, planning the designs, painting the walls, and getting the supplies together—it really feels great to actually stencil. It is by far the easiest part of the project and provides instantly gratifying results: as soon as the first design appears on the wall, the room begins to change—it suddenly looks colorful and *lively*.

To put up the first design, pick the spot where you want to begin and attach the stencil to the wall with two or three pieces of masking tape. Dip the brush into the paint and wipe away any excess on the lip of the container. Holding the brush in one hand and keeping the stencil flat with the other, paint the first few strokes in the center of the design to get rid of even more paint. When only a little paint remains on the brush, start painting at the edges of the cutout—

away from the edge and toward the middle of the design. Use short strokes. If the design consists mainly of slits or slots (line drawings) and there is no open space in the middle, make your brush fairly dry by wiping excess paint on a piece of scrap paper. Run the brush quickly along the cutout lines of the design and try not to bump it into the end. Always direct the brush toward the middle of a line.

Put the brush in water when you're through painting. Leave the stencil where it is and check the color carefully to make sure that it doesn't need another coat—you won't really know until the paint dries. To remove the stencil, lift the tape from the wall. Step back and admire your work. Wipe away any paint that might have collected on the back of the stencil with your fingers, a cloth, or a paper towel. The pieces of tape should still be attached to the stencil—they enable you to stick and restick it to the wall over and over.

Stencil one color at a time: carry one color of a border all the way around the room before introducing the second color. Other labor- and timesaving tips: apply paint from the right to the left side of the stencil if you're moving a border stencil from left to right—the paint will dry on the right side first, minimizing your chances of smudging when you move and re-attach the stencil. If the various cutouts are so close together that you can't keep your brush out of the wrong holes, cover them with tape so that paint can't get through (but don't mask all the holes, or you won't have any windows to help you in positioning). Remove the tape very carefully to avoid ripping the stencil. Prevent future problems by remembering that after acrylic dries (too quickly!), it is permanent. Keep lids on paint jars when they are not in use. Don't let brushes dry out with paint in them—keep them in the water jar until you can wash them thoroughly with warm water and soap. Clean up any accidents right away with a wet cloth or paper towel—little blobs that fall on woodwork or floor come up easily when wet; when dry, you have to scrape. Acrylic can never be removed from fabrics. Dress for the occasion and protect carpeting and upholstery unless you know that you are a dripless wonder. If paint builds up in the cutout parts of the stencil to the extent that the images degrade (or shrink!), cut it away with the X-acto knife. Holding the stencil in front of you, pare away dried paint as if you were peeling fruit.

Plates 48, 49, 50, 51, and 52. Stenciling in progress.

BORDERS

If you stencil a border that wraps around a room, you'll find that you can't fit the stiff, unyielding stencil into the corners. There are several ways to handle this problem, most of which require cutting the stencil to make it fit. The method that I like best produces a continuous band of design that encircles the room and does not appear to stop and start in the corners. Begin by stenciling along the wall, skipping all the corners as you pass them. Make sure to leave enough space for the designs but don't put them in until after you stencil in all the colors elsewhere and you can cut up the stencil.

Sometimes (believe it or not) a room works out so that the same part of the design is missing from each corner (fig. 5-1), and you have to cut the stencil only once to make it fit (fig. 5-2). Tape the stencil into the corner and paint each side, putting in all the colors at once. If the corners don't work out similarly, you may have to cut the stencil differently for each one. Cut the stencil and do the first corner. Tape it back together again to recut if necessary and stencil in the second, third, and fourth corners. Your stencil probably contains enough repetitions of the design so that you don't have to cut up the same piece over and over, and in most cases an approximate fit in the corners is quite sufficient—it hardly matters if a pineapple is 1″ farther to the right in one corner than it is elsewhere. You should try to average the cuts—you won't have to make so many.

When all the corners are stenciled and the design wrapped around the room, an odd space may be left over where the end meets the beginning. You can either run the end into the beginning (which looks fine more often than you might think) or fill the space with something else. You can letter in your name and the date or drop in an unrelated design that matches those in the border in size and color: a sleeping cat, a bunch of flowers, a sailboat, watermelon, or whatever you want (fig. 5-3).

Plate 53. Some borders abut casually.

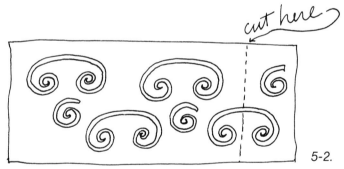

5-2.

5-1.

84

Plate 54. Living room, Boulder, Colorado.

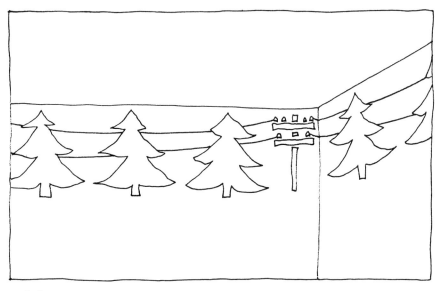

5-3.

Another way to handle borders in corners produces a result similar to wallpaper—the design breaks off sharply in each corner but is spliced together neatly enough so that it remains visually an unbroken band. Trim the left side of the stencil so that the design fits as flush as possible into the corner on the left side. Begin stenciling from the far left of the wall and go as far into the next corner as you can. Stop there and resume at the next wall, again fitting the stencil into the corner so that the design begins as far to the left as possible. Go around the room until you make a full circle. You end up with a border with interruptions only at the far right of each wall. Pick the wall with the biggest interruption and trim the stencil so that the design fits right up to the corner (fig. 5-4). Stencil in the corner, doing all the colors at once. Pick the wall with the next largest interruption and cut the stencil again to fit that corner. Repeat until all the corners are finished.

Another corner treatment involves making an entirely new stencil that folds vertically in the middle and fits right into a corner (fig. 5-5). Stencil board is hard to fold, so you should make your corner stencil of bristol board. Stencil the corners first and then stencil the rest of the border as usual, beginning on the left side of every wall. You can also begin the border in the middle of each wall and stencil out to the corners. The centering method is especially effective in a truly rectangular or square room: the borders are symmetrical and the opposite walls match.

Plate 55. Dining area, Vail, Colorado.

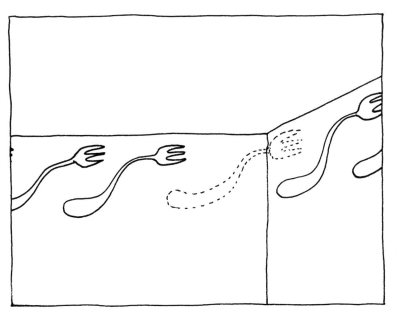

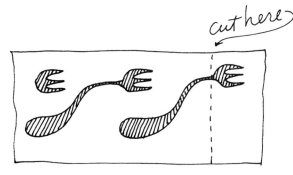

5-4.

If the border designs are very small and numerous, you can probably fit the stencil quite close to the corners. If the designs are large and widely spaced, you can leave larger spaces at the corners without detracting from the design. In either case border tricks may be unnecessary.

Windows and doors feature an entirely different kind of corner, and it can be equally tricky to run borders smoothly around them. Suppose that the border design is a twining vine: you can either stencil the horizontal and vertical sections until they meet in the corners (fig. 5-6) or ease the stencil gradually around each corner, painting in pieces of the border bit by bit until it turns a complete 90 degrees (fig. 5-7). You can also paint in the vine freehand as it turns the corner instead of manipulating the stencil and coloring in fits and starts. Just stencil up to each turning point, leave a blank, turn the stencil 90 degrees, and resume the border. Go back later and connect the stems with a curving line of the right color.

5-6.

5-7.

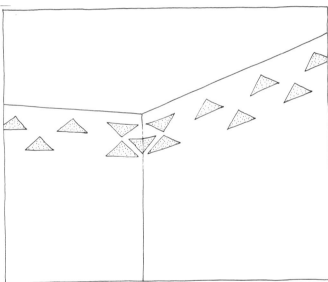

5-5.

If a border consists of unconnected designs, you can often space it around the corner. Paint in the straight sections, leaving the corners blank, then put into them whatever border designs seem to fit (fig. 5-8). Another alternative is to stop the borders abruptly at the ends of the window or door frame. The corners will be completely empty of design, and you can drop a new, even unrelated design into them. It should be about the same width and the same colors (fig. 5-9).

Tricks with tape can make very neat corners, but they tend to look fussy, especially if the designs are informal, free, and flowing. I use tape only to stencil solid, formal bands or borders in which the designs are rigidly and regularly spaced. You can either miter the corners like the molding in a picture frame or square them off.

To miter with tape, measure the distance from the window frame to the outside edge of the border and draw a line that extends the edge well into the corner (fig. 5-10). Do the same for the other side of the corner (fig. 5-11). These intersecting lines establish the outside edge of the 90-degree angle that the border forms in the corner. To establish the diagonal line of the miter, draw a line from the penciled corner to the actual corner (fig. 5-12). Run a piece of masking tape along this line, either above or below it (fig. 5-13). Do *not* cover the line with tape. If you placed the masking tape above the line, you can stencil in the bottom half of the corner. Put the stencil in place so that the bottom designs fit over those already stenciled below it and the top designs (as yet unstenciled) reach up to the tape. Stencil in the designs up to the tape (fig. 5-14).

5-8.

5-9.

88

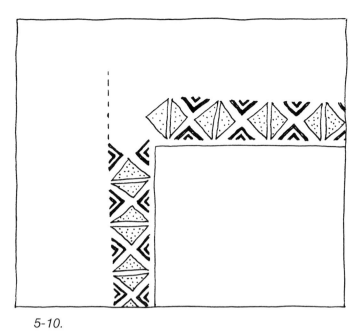

5-10.

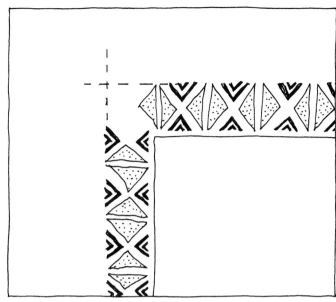

5-11.

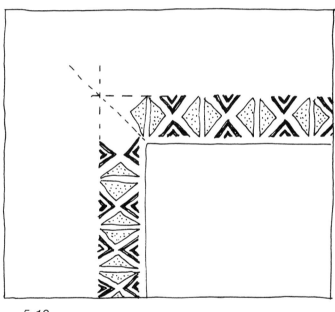

5-12.

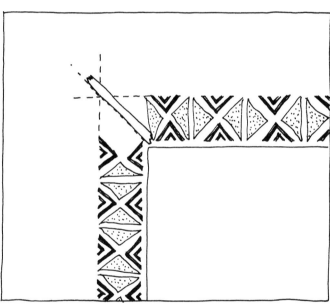

5-13.

5-14.

5-15.

5-16.

Lift the stencil and move the tape to the other side of the line. Stencil in the top half of the corner, making sure that the designs reach all the way to the tape. When you remove the stencil and tape, you will have a relentlessly crisp corner (fig. 5-15).

To square off a corner, extend the outside edges of the border so that they meet in the corners—just as for mitering. Instead of connecting the corners with a diagonal line, however, run pieces of masking tape along the outside edges of the penciled lines at the corner. The tape enforces the right angle of the corner onto the stenciling. Run either the vertical or horizontal section of the border into the corner and stop the design at the tape (fig. 5-16).

STRIPES AND INDIVIDUAL DESIGNS

If a stencil includes spaces to establish the proper distance between it and its neighbors, the result is automatic spacing of designs. If you are working with stripes, decide how far apart you want the stripes to be and stencil in the first stripe from floor to ceiling at the far-left side of the wall. Measure the correct distance between that stripe and the next and tape the stencil in place to begin the next stripe. Cut a piece of bristol board that extends from the left edge of the stencil to the right edge of the first stripe and tape it to the stencil. The stencil is now of the proper width to space itself. You can stencil stripes exactly the same distance apart, stripe by stripe, mile after mile, without ever measuring again or making a single mark on the wall.

If you want to stencil individual designs between rows of stripes, attach paper flanges to the stencil that extend to the stripe on the left and to the design below. If there are no stripes to guide the placement of individual designs, measure and mark their locations on the wall. A tiny penciled mark then appears in the open middle of a stencil, signaling that it is in the correct position. If the stencil has a solid center that doesn't permit a view of the mark, cut a little window in it just large enough for a peek. If the marks show after the work is done, you can paint over them.

You're bound to make a mistake occasionally—in measuring, in positioning—and you're bound to change your mind. What if you turn out not to like mitered corners, for example? This is one occasion that you saved your background paint for. You can cover mistakes in minutes and be ready to stencil again in only an hour or so.

FINISHING

While you work, you think of things to do when you're finished; when you *are* finished, you forget all about them until everything's been put away; so don't put your stuff away too soon. Go around the room and paint over unwanted ties with appropriate colors. Cover any smears, runs, blobs, and pencil marks. Paint in parts that you forgot—a left-out leaf, curlicue, or whatever. If there are some details that you wanted to paint in by hand—eyes, spots, claws, little gold stripes, highlights—do them. Then put your stuff away.

Give yourself and your family a few days to look over the walls. When you're sure that you don't want to add or subtract anything, you can varnish them. Use polyurethane—flat, satin, or glossy—and apply it with a nylon brush. If you have no particular reason to varnish the walls, don't. I use varnish in bathrooms and kitchens—wherever there's high humidity, dirt, or grease and whenever I think that a glossy surface would enhance the designs. I have yet to put varnish on a single wall in my own house, however, and none shows the slightest wear.

Plate 57. Ceiling, Denver Botanic Gardens.

Plate 56. Construction-paper models taped to wall.

91

Plate 58. Medicine chest.

CHAPTER 6:

PROJECTS

It has probably occurred to you that you can apply stencils to other things besides walls. This chapter describes stenciling on floors, ceilings, doors, window shades, furniture, folding screens, and floorcloths. Children also enjoy stenciling, and for them there are a few projects on paper. With a nice design, some paint and a reasonably flat surface you can stencil on just about anything from lunchboxes to bathtubs.

FLOORS

A cautionary note: doing anything to a floor is a big drag. You probably shouldn't stencil a floor until you've acquired enough experience to do it fast—even under the best conditions it can take two or three weeks. If you have a terrible floor, especially one that's been painted before and that's located in an out-of-the-way place (the sewing room), it is a candidate for a first floor-stenciling attempt.

There is a large selection of design traditions to choose from in planning a floor. Two obvious choices involve the structure of floors themselves: tiles and inlaid wood. To imitate a tile floor, you can design stencils within a square (or diamond, hexagon, triangle) format to produce a network of continuous design. Around the outside you might plan a border, perhaps simple in form and color in which to enclose the busier allover pattern. Some tile designs are simple in themselves, of course. Imagine that your individual tiles are 12″ (32 cm) across: you can confine your design to 4″ (11 cm) in the center, leaving 6″ (16 cm) of empty space around it. Another tile pattern alter-

nates colors in a checkerboard, negative-positive manner. Half the squares might be blue with yellow centers, and half yellow with blue centers. Although floral and geometric designs are the most obvious choices for the centers, it would be fun to use incongruous images such as Sunkist lemons (have a rubber stamp made for the brand name) or animals. To make sure that tile designs look their best, measure very carefully so that no squares are truncated by walls and the design fits perfectly on the floor.

Inlaid-wood designs usually involve checkered or herringbone parquet patterns. Plan such conventional designs in unconventional colors: peach and mint green, for example, or turquoise and yellow.

Consider an oriental, Navaho, or Chinese rug floor. For oriental or Chinese designs plan borders around the perimeter: a large major border and some smaller ones. Make up designs for the middle section and position them according to the conventions of rug making (consult books at the library). Use your favorite rug design as is or combine several rugs. Some oriental rugs consist of little more than a central medallion or group of medallions surrounded by borders. These and the simpler Navaho rugs are the easiest to imitate. Chinese rugs, because of their restraint in color and design, are also easy to copy—and easy to live with.

Most floor designs are somewhat formal and should be planned very carefully. Do your best measuring, not neglecting the placement of heat registers and other impediments, and transfer the proportions to graph paper. Xerox the floor plan so that you can try many different designs at the same time.

To prepare a floor for stenciling, remove wax. If the floor is glossy, sand it lightly. Use liquid sandpaper, which you wipe or brush on, or an electric sander. Fill bad cracks in the floor and sand the filler after it dries. Paint the floor with flat or satin oil-based enamel. After you apply the background coat, lay masking tape to paint in the borders. If the painted surface is flat or satin, you can use acrylics to apply the designs—they bond nicely with the surface. If you used glossy enamel, you can stencil the designs with spray enamels or treat the surface with liquid sandpaper. Just brush it on through the stencil and, when it is dry, apply the color over it. If possible, work from one end of the room to the other to avoid excess traffic on the unvarnished, vulnerable stenciling. Wear soft clothes—no rivets—and sweat socks to walk over a freshly stenciled surface. Stencil the borders first and then the inside of the floor.

If the limited range of colors doesn't discourage you, you can save some time by stenciling with spray enamels, even on a nonglossy surface. The image is softened slightly by the spray, but that doesn't usually matter on floors. Hold the stencil as flat as possible on the floor to inhibit wandering spray. Cover in light coats: the spray dries very quickly, and you can apply a second coat almost immediately. Wipe the stencil assiduously with a lightly turpentined rag. Although the designs may look as if they need extra coats of paint, make sure that they really do by lifting the stencil and contrasting the sprayed design with the background. Without brush marks to betray you, you

can get by with less paint.

Give the floor two or three coats of polyurethane varnish. The glossy type enhances bright colors; satin is less brassy-looking; flat may be too dull. Resist the temptation to sand between coats—you might erase your stenciling. Don't replace heavy pieces of furniture until a week or two after the last coat of varnish. Varnish continues to harden long after it feels dry.

CEILINGS

There is no painless way to stencil on the ceiling. That fact alone is a sufficient argument against choosing a complicated, intricate design for a first effort. A simple border around the perimeter or a central medallion is a relatively easy and promising approach to ceiling decoration. Round or oval medallions can either substitute for or enhance central light fixtures. To make ordinary designs into circular compositions, arrange them into a curved border—a continuous line of designs—that eventually closes and forms a circle (fig. 6-1). You can also place design elements so that they radiate out from a central point (fig. 6-2). For border ideas look at the pressed-tin ceilings that were so popular in old buildings. At least one modern manufacturer publishes a catalog full of photos and drawings of designs—borders, repeating tile compositions, medallions, and rectangular panels. In planning a border, regardless of the source of the design, remember that the more widely spaced the elements are, the easier they are to apply.

Plate 59. Bedroom ceiling with sloping wall, Boulder, Colorado.

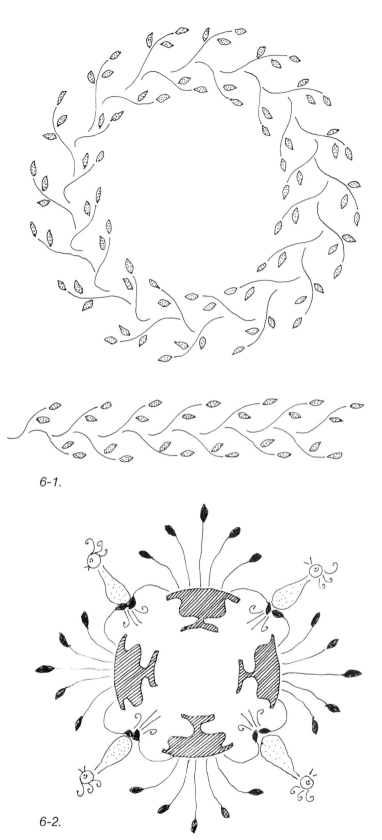

6-1.

6-2.

You probably won't need scaffolding to work around the perimeter of a ceiling: you can lean against the nearby wall while standing on a ladder. To work in the middle of the ceiling, you'll certainly need a scaffold: they come in heights 5′ (1.5 m) and up and are available from rental places. If your ceiling hasn't been installed yet, you might be able to stencil it in advance. If you plan on having acoustical tiles, you can stencil them one by one, comfortably seated at a table. Apply designs with a brush (unless you're seated): spray cans won't work in a horizontal, upside-down position. Don't bother varnishing a stenciled ceiling—it receives little wear.

DOORS

Doors are really fun to stencil—the contours of an ordinary paneled door present a ready-made composition of vertical panels, borders of varying widths, and wide horizontal spaces. You might do the flat planes around the panels in one color, the panels themselves in a different color, and the strips of molding around the panels in one or two different colors. You can stencil unpaneled doors to imitate paneled ones: try different-colored rectangles to represent panels and small bands of color around them to represent molding. Or, taking advantage of the open space, you can plan a large central medallion, wide vertical stripes, or even an allover pattern for the door. Rug designs make great doors.

Since a door presents a small, rather contained area for decoration, feel free to splurge with color. Use the designs to create an orderly composition and to tie together the many different areas in a paneled door but use color unrestrainedly if you want to, especially if you've hidden your light under a bushel with the walls. I love to work with dark colors—deep tones over a dark, rich field—and a door may offer the only opportunity in a room in which you want to use the walls to bounce the light around.

Before you begin work on a door, make sure that the surface will take the paint. If it is covered with shiny old varnish or enamel, cut the gloss with liquid or regular sandpaper. If it is unfinished, prime before painting. Use latex, enamel, or acrylic paint. Mask with tape to make straight lines, unless the molding and a steady hand enable you to do without. Apply the stenciling as you would on a wall and use the appropriate polyurethane finish: flat, satin, or glossy. Glossy varnish looks great on a door: it makes dark colors look as if they were underwater.

WINDOW SHADES

Window shades are a terrific solution to a common problem. They never get in the way; they roll up and disappear when you want to let light in; they can be either translucent or opaque; they come in a wide range of colors; they never look pompous or heavy; and, best of all, they fit neatly into the window frame without covering up nearby stenciled borders. I like light, delicate designs for window shades, particularly if the shade is translucent and light shines through the colors. Plan the design so that you don't have to unroll the entire shade to see it. A vertical or diagonal stripe or any allover repeating pattern looks great on window shades. Stencil on white or colored linen-type shades. Avoid cheap plastic shades, which take paint poorly and don't even work very well.

Work on the floor. Unroll the shade and put a heavy object near the wooden dowel to keep the shade from rolling itself up. You'll probably have to tame the curl at the other end with a few more heavy objects. You can work directly on the shade: no priming or other preparation is necessary. Apply the paint somewhat thinly—you don't want it to crack off with the movement of the shade. Thin paint also produces a translucent effect that is appealing in a window shade.

Acrylics are the best choice—they can be quite translucent, and they stay flexible even when dry. When the stenciling is done, roll the shade up by hand. It it now ready for you to install and use. Don't varnish: you can safely wash the screen with warm water and a sponge. If you've never washed a window shade before, however, it is unlikely that you'll ever want to.

FURNITURE

The furniture that I've stenciled consists of pieces of junk that I bought cheap and had stripped and reglued if necessary. I never buy anything that's warped, split, or seriously deformed. The fact that I work on one-at-a-time pieces makes it hard for me to formulate rules about furniture decoration. I tend to avoid bamboo etageres in favor of simply designed and constructed pieces with many flat planes. If the idea of snooping around garage sales and antique stores looking for flat-planed, sturdy tables doesn't do much for you, consider the ubiquitous unfinished-furniture stores. They offer an entire collection of very simply designed, new furniture that is completely free of distracting adornment of any kind. You can buy a footstool to practice on and move up to chests of drawers when you acquire more confidence.

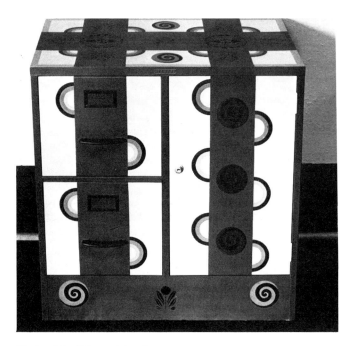

Plate 60. File cabinet.

Plate 61. Detail of file cabinet.

C-5. Stenciled door.

C-6. Plant stand.

C-7. T-shirt.

99

C-8, C-9, C-10, and C-11. Dining room, Boulder,
Colorado.

C-12. Porch, Boulder, Colorado.

C-13. Porch detail, Boulder, Colorado.

C-14. Model room, May D & F, Denver, Colorado.

C-15. Detail of model room.

C-16. Detail of powder room, Denver, Colorado.

C-17. Bedroom, Boulder, Colorado.

Treat the planes of the furniture (the top surface, front, sides, sometimes legs) individually and design your compositions to suit them. A table, for example, calls for a unified, coherent design that fills the top surface. Unless the legs are prominently wide or square, you'll want to stop there, but the leg (or pedestal) of a plant stand is an intrinsic part of the design, deserving almost as much attention as the top. Some pieces are *all* surface—a file cabinet, for instance—and you may decide to decorate every plane. The designs should flow together, unifying all the surfaces, but each plane should also work as an individual composition. The top of most pieces is the most important surface: you might want to plan on extra design and color. Intricacy and fineness of detail enhance furniture stenciling. I like to hand-paint some of the details. I often use gold, which seems to clarify and brighten all of the designs around it.

Preparation is the same for both stripped and unfinished furniture. Always sand the piece and prime it with oil-based primer: the primer seals the wood and creates a clean, paintable surface to work on. It may also reveal cracks for you to fill; sand the filled cracks and prime them. You may need to resand after priming: it depends on the type of wood and how smooth you want it. Use latex or acrylic paint for the background color. Use masking tape for straight lines, as usual.

If you plan any gold detail (which you can also use on walls), buy Pelikan gold ink at an art-supply store. Apply the gold detail—or any other detail—with a fine brush: a #1 to #00 in the Winsor-Newton designer series, perhaps. The usual choice of varnishes awaits you at the end of the project. My particular favorite is glossy, but there's no practical reason to choose it over the others. You must varnish furniture with something, however, and you can cover the top with a piece of glass, cut to size and smoothed around the edges, at a glass store.

FOLDING SCREENS

Some people live in large spaces that combine the functions of living room, dining room, and study. A screen provides a change of scene at dinner or sections off a bit of privacy for the person at the desk. A three-panel screen is wide enough for most purposes. The panels should be narrow enough to prevent flexing and short enough for an adult head to peep over the top. I recently made a three-panel screen with twelve stretcher bars from an art-supply store. Put together, they formed a three-part rectangle 66″ (about 175 cm) tall and 78″ (about 200 cm) wide. These proportions worked very well for composing designs.

Plate 62. Half-round table.

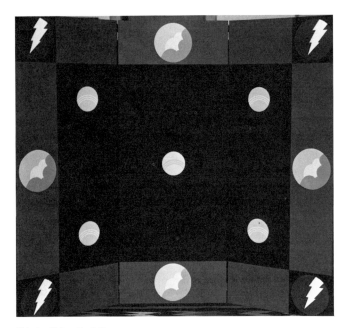

Plate 63. Folding screen.

Plate 64. Detail of folding screen.

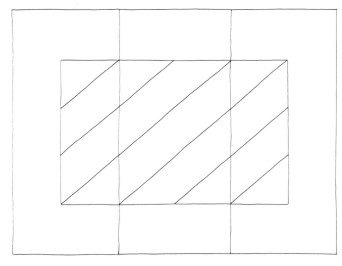

6-3.

You might want to begin your design with a border running all the way around the perimeter of the panel group (fig. 6-3). It ties the panels together and makes it easier for you to plan a design for the inside space. Fill it with diagonal, vertical, or horizontal stripes or any field of repeating designs. For specific designs consult quilts, carpets (oriental, Chinese, American Indian), Japanese family crests, Japanese stenciled paper, or early American wall stencils. Trellis patterns also work nicely on screens. You can stencil little repeating designs in the middle of each square or diamond-shaped pane.

Buy twelve stretchers from an art-supply store, six 66" (176 cm) long and six 26" (68 cm) long; 24 chips to go with them; and a quart of gesso. At a paint store you can buy a wonderful little tool called a poly-brush that costs less than a dollar and looks like a popsicle—a piece of sponge on a stick. You should also have a yardstick, a carpenter's square, a hammer, a staple gun and boxes of staples, a pair of scissors, and a queen-sized sheet. If you want the screen to be translucent, get a plain white or pastel sheet; if it's to be opaque, the sheet can be covered with printed designs, since you'll never see them again.

To assemble the four stretchers into a panel, push the corners together. The ends of the individual stretcher-bar lengths are specially cut with flanges and grooves. To form a right angle, you merely line up the flanges and grooves and ease them together. Check for a perfect right angle with your carpenter's square: lay the tool over the corner and, if the corners match, insert the little wooden chips (two for each corner) into the slots in the angle to help stabilize the corner. If the angles don't match, adjust the stretchers until they do. Proceed in this fashion until all four corners are fitted together and secure. You might as well do all of the panels at once. Check every angle. If you have trouble fitting flanges into grooves at some of the corners, a few taps with the hammer will make them go together.

Cut the queen-size sheet into three pieces by spreading it out on the lawn or the workroom floor and laying the assembled panels on top of it. You need a little extra material for each panel—3" (8 cm) or so on each side to wrap around the stretcher bars. Space the frames accordingly on the sheets and cut around them with the scissors. Put aside two of the frames and two of the pieces of sheet.

Wet the third piece of sheet (with the hose or in the sink, depending on where you are) and lay the panel over it. Staple once in the middle of one of the long sides, placing the staple on the side away from the sheet—you wrap the sheet around the panel and do all of the stapling on the back side. Insert the second staple opposite the first in the middle of the other long side. As you apply this staple, pull the material taut. Measure the distance across the panel to avoid pulling the material too taut and caving in the sides of the panel. Apply the third staple in the middle of one of the short sides; apply the fourth opposite it. Pull the material somewhat taut while putting in the third staple, tauter while putting in the fourth. Put successive staples every 2″ or 3″ (5 or 7.5 cm) across the short sides, pulling the material taut each time (fig. 6-4). Staple along one of the long sides. Keep the amount of wraparound material even—if it extends 2″ (5 cm) beyond the middle staple, make sure that it extends 2″ beyond the others. Place the staples 2″ or 3″ (5 or 7.5 cm) apart. Staple along the opposite side. Pull the sheet taut, continually measuring to make certain that the distance across the middle of the panel remains the same as at the ends. Make the corners of the panel neat by tucking and flattening the sheet, as in making a bed (hospital corners!), and folding it around one side to be stapled flat.

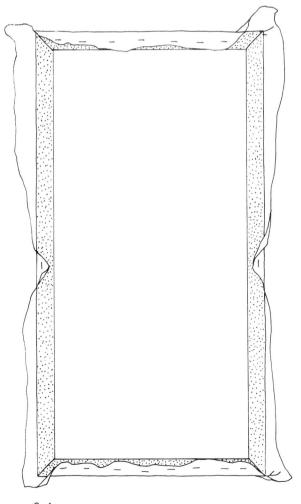

6-4.

If the sheet is still damp, you should gesso it right away. If not, dampen it again (a spritz with the hose, a onceover with a wet sponge). Thin some gesso with water—a bit less water than gesso—and brush it on the stretched sheet with the polybrush. Do not press into the sheet with the brush (no scrubbing either). Don't gesso the outside edges of the panel yet. Put the panel aside to dry and stretch and gesso the next panel.

When the first panel is dry, sand it very lightly with medium sandpaper. Apply a new coat of thinned gesso to the dry panel. Dry, sand, and gesso until the panels are as smooth as you want them. Some texture—of the fabric weave—might be desirable: it looks like crepe. Give the panel a coat of gesso on the reverse side as well to ensure that no paint will come through and ruin the design on the front. Three coats of gesso should be sufficient, fewer for a translucent screen— just make sure that no tiny holes are left in the weave and that the surface is as you like it. After all the panels are gessoed, you may find that the sheet has warped or buckled slightly near the edges. Take out the staples in the affected area and restretch. Very subtle adjustments are usually all you need—in fact, if you pull too hard on the sheet, you'll make waves elsewhere. Pull gently and watch the edges carefully.

Use latex, if possible, to paint in the background color. Put it on with a polybrush or a wide painter's brush. Use latex for the borders and the panel edges as well, unless they are quite narrow. Measure carefully and use masking tape to define the straight lines. Apply the rest of the designs in the usual way with acrylic and stencils. To finish the back sides of the panels, paint the stapled fabric on the backs of the stretcher bars with thinned Elmer's glue or gesso to hold it flat. When the glue has dried, trim away excess fabric with an X-acto knife. Paint the backs of the panels with latex. You can either paint everything one color or paint the stretcher frames and the sheet backs contrasting colors. Put designs on the backs of the panels if you want to: both sides of the screen will probably be visible most of the time. When you've finished painting, varnish both sides. Use flat, satin, or glossy polyurethane. One coat should suffice.

To fasten the three panels together into a folding screen, buy four folding-screen hinges at a hardware store. They come in a ¾″ (19 mm) width, which is exactly right for the thickness of the stretcher frames. Like little magic tricks, they open in two directions and are guaranteed to dazzle your friends. Follow the instructions on the package to install them, making sure that you attach all of them at the same height.

FLOORCLOTHS

Floorcloths are like linoleum rugs—stiff, smooth, slightly comical, brightly colored, and shiny. They bear up well under traffic, and you can vacuum and mop them just like linoleum. Use a 3'-×-5' (0.9-×-1.5 m) floorcloth just as you would an area rug. When you become experienced with the materials and techniques, you might like to try larger floorcloths—perhaps even wall-to-wallers. The preparation of the canvas takes a long time, however: be content with a 3'-×-5' for starters.

Many rugs come in a three-by-five or similar format. Oriental prayer rugs and Navaho rugs would be obvious choices for inspiration. I see in my mind's eye floorcloths covered with colorful geometric designs of Caucasian rugs or flat-woven kilims, old eye-dazzlers and Germantown Navahos. Rug designs from Guatemala and Mexico work well, as do the crewel flora and fauna of East Indian rugs. The fascinating geometrical designs of early American pieced quilts make superior floorcloths now, just as they did in 1800. Modern painting (Frank Stella, Max Bill, Paul Feeley) can provide abstract floorcloth inspiration, as can molas, the appliquéd-fabric compositions from San Blas. Tesselated designs (tile patterns) make a good basis for floorcloth designs. Checkerboard tiles, parquet designs, or Islamic floral motifs all work very well.

To get down to it, go to an art-supply store and buy the heaviest canvas available (14-ounce weight at least), 3' (0.9 m) wide and 5½' (1.6 m) long. If you become a floorcloth freak, investigate *very* heavy canvas—some of the large canvas-supply places in New York do mail-order business, and you can find their addresses in the Manhattan Yellow Pages in the library. Buy four stretchers—two 5' (1.5 m) and two 3' (0.9 m)—and a quart of Liquitex gesso. You also need a staple gun, pushpins, masking tape, brushes, and paint.

Assemble the stretchers as you would for a folding-screen panel. Thoroughly soak the canvas in water to get rid of creases and folds. You might even have to iron it. Wet the canvas again before stretching: it shrinks while drying and becomes quite taut. Follow the stapling order described in the folding-screen section with this difference: attach the long-side staples to the top of the stretcher right on the face of the floorcloth. At the short ends you can wrap the canvas around the stretcher and apply the staples to the sides or back of the frame. Rewet the canvas and apply a coat of thinned gesso. If the canvas isn't too rough, you can use the wonderful polybrush. If it is,

you'll have to use a conventional paint-store brush.

Sand the surface when the gesso is dry and regesso. Sand and regresso two more times. Take out the side staples after the canvas has had an opportunity to dry flat a few times and replace them with pushpins. Remove the pushpins during subsequent coats of gesso. Cover the staple scars with gesso and move the pushpins to different spots to prevent them from making scars. Keep sanding and gessoing until the canvas is about 1/16" (1.5 mm) thick and fairly smooth.

Paint in the background colors for the field and border with latex. Use tape to make straight lines or to define stripes. Stencil on the cloth in the usual way. Apply three or four coats of polyurethane. I love glossy for floorcloths: they acquire a wonderful wet look, and they're easy to wash with soap and water. After a great deal of heavy traffic the gloss will fade somewhat. You can either renew it with a new coat of varnish or simply enjoy the duller sheen. Never sand between coats of polyurethane—even though the label instructions recommend it.

After you remove the floorcloth from the stretcher, you can either cut off the raw canvas that was wrapped around the end bars or hem the piece by folding the raw canvas underneath and gluing it to the back of the cloth. A third alternative is to trim the raw ends of the canvas to within 2" (5.1 cm) or so of the painting and to unravel the weft strands, making a canvas fringe for the cloth.

Don't use a floorcloth on top of carpeting—the pressure of traffic puts too much strain on the fibers. Use it on wood floors, linoleum, tiles, or concrete. If the cloth slips, tack it down here and there with small pieces of double-sided carpet tape. Carpet tape will also keep the corners from curling up if that's a problem.

STENCILING ON PAPER

If you live with older children (no three-year-olds will appreciate this), you can do some nice things with them on paper; you might even make something useful. Wrapping paper is easy and fun to decorate. Use kraft paper, white or solid-color wrapping tissue, large sheets of plain newsprint, or white shelf paper. The children can draw designs on stencil paper, and you can cut them out if you don't want them wielding knives. Encourage the kids to make simple shapes. They might like to trace cookie cutters, animal crackers, leaves, small change, or puzzle pieces. They will soon think of their own things to trace—maybe parts of their bodies such as hands and feet.

The stencils for wrapping paper do not need to be

cut on stencil board. Any sturdy paper will do for this casual, few-times use. Let the kids stencil with watercolor or, if they're very responsible, with acrylic, which eventually washes off skin but sticks to clothing. Not only children can make wrapping paper: you can make it too, but yours will be a lot neater and the kids might be jealous.

You and your kids can also make notepaper. A great paper to use is tinted charcoal paper. The colors are gorgeous, and the paper has a very classy texture. Cut 7"-×-6¼" (17.7-×-15.8 cm) pieces by hand or with a paper cutter. Folded once in the middle, they will fit neatly into a standard-size envelope. In choosing colors for notepaper pay attention to contrast: if you decide to stencil a large design smack in the middle of the page, make sure that the intensity of the color is similar to that of the paper. The greatest visual contrast must occur between the message and the paper, not between the design and the paper. If you're limiting your design to a border, you can indulge in stronger contrast. You can also stencil on postcards and en-

velopes. Get stamped postcards from the post office or make them out of heavy paper like bristol board. A nice place to put a design on an envelope is on the gummed edge where people used to put sealing wax. The design breaks up when the envelope is opened.

Plate 66. Stenciled paper and envelopes.

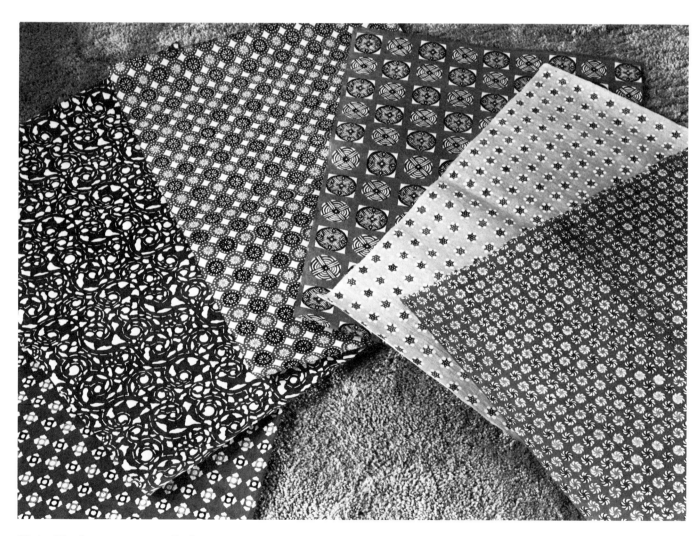

Plate 65. Japanese stenciled paper.

If the kids rave for more, you can stencil three-dimensional objects. The barrel-shaped cardboard containers from which ice cream is dispensed make nice wastebaskets or canisters. Paint them first with gesso or latex, then apply the background color and the stenciled decoration and varnish. Boxes from a liquor store with interior dividers appeal to children and other people with a cubbyhole instinct. Prime them for painting with gesso or latex, paint, stencil, and varnish.

BATHTUBS, LUNCHBOXES, AND T-SHIRTS

I once stenciled a bathtub for a friend, and it was pretty much like stenciling anything else. The tub had feet and curving sides and bottom. I made my stencil out of bristol board—stencil board is too stiff—so that it would conform to the curve somewhat. The tub had already been painted; I merely applied the design to the outside of the tub with acrylics. As far as I know, the tub was never varnished. The design still exists, looking just as it did on the day it was born. I've wondered about stenciling on the inside of a tub but have not had the occasion to try it.

I bought my son the wrong lunchbox one year. I forget what design it had, but it was *not* the *Star Trek* lunchbox that he wanted. He used it for about a year but balked the following September—he would not go through another grade with the wrong lunchbox. We consulted about designs, and he decided to have bi-planes in white and red against a blue field. We sanded the old lunchbox—it was rusty—and sprayed it inside and out with blue enamel. I made the stencil from a drawing. I painted the design with enamel from the paint shelf. It wore well—at least as well as the original.

A T-shirt store in Boulder, Colorado silk-screens designs onto the shirts that they sell. I brought in a stencil one day and asked them to put the design on a purple T-shirt. They said that the stencil was too heavy, so I made another out of graph tracing paper (the only light paper that I happened to have at home). They were dubious about stenciling one color on top of another—I wanted yellow stripes on a red wasp—but they tried it anyway. The T-shirt looked beautiful and it still does, though I must admit that I take pains with it—it has never seen the inside of a drier nor felt the sting of a hot-water wash.

I've thought of stenciling on skin too.

Plate 67. Bathtub.

CHAPTER 7:

FULL - SIZE DESIGNS
FOR TRACING

This chapter contains 27 full-size designs ready for tracing, ranging from geometrics to florals, Victorian to Japanese motifs. I hope that they spur you to create many more exciting stencils of your own!

7-2.

7-3.

7-4.

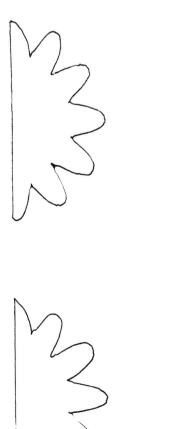

7-5.

114

7-6.

7-7.

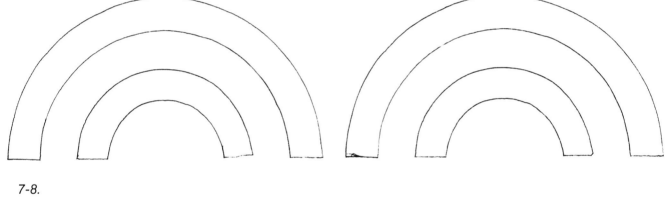

7-8.

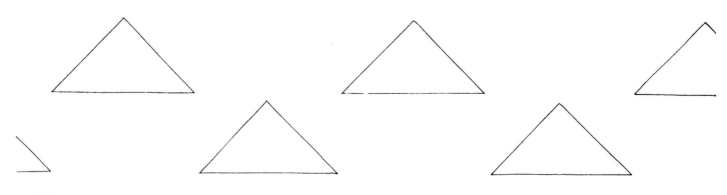

7-9.

7-10.

7-11.

7-14.

7-15.

Greek/Victorian border

7-16.

African design

7-17.

124

Victorian
designs

7-18.

Victorian
borders

7-19.

7-20.

Japanese
gingko
leaf

7-21.

7-22.

7-23.

7-24.

7-25.

7-26.

Victorian

early
American
flower

7-27.

INDEX

Numbers in italics refer to illustrative matter.

abutting colors, 22, *23*
acrylic paints, 79–80, 81, 95, 96, 105, 107, 109, 110
African folk art, design motifs from, 53, *54*, 56
amusements, nonsporting, design motifs from, *52*–53
animals as design motifs, *see also* bugs; fish; horses, 36, *37*, *44–47*, *50*–51, 53
architectural ornamentation, design motifs from, *43*
art deco, 8–9, 58
art nouveau, 8, 58
art of other cultures, design motifs from, 53–*57*, 93, 106, 108
Associated Artists, 8
asymmetrical designs:
    multicolored, 20–*23*
    transfer of, to stencil board, 15
Audsley, W. and G., 58

ballet, design motifs from, 51
basic design, 11–13
baskets, design motifs from, 53, *55*, 58
bathtubs, *110*
bilaterally symmetrical designs, 14
billboards, design motifs from, *41–42*
borders and stripes, 13, *24–28*, 61–*63*, 74, 76, 79, 96
    for ceilings, 94
    corner treatment, *84–90*
    design motifs for, *31*, *33*, *37*, *47*, *54*
    for floors, 93
    for folding screens, 106
    for formal rooms, 71
    for larger rooms, 70
    multicolored, 26
    for notepaper, 109
    for smaller rooms, 71
    spacing of designs, 26, *27*
    wall stenciling and, *84–91*
bouquet shapes, design motifs from, 33
bristol board, 81, 86, 90, 110
bugs, design motifs from, 36, *37–38*
buildings, *see also* houses, 41

cabinets, kitchen, 76
candlestick shapes, design motifs from, *33*
canvas for floorcloth, 108
carbon paper, 15

ceilings, *94–95*
chair-rail moldings, 62–*63*, 74, 79
chair shapes, design motifs from, *34*
Chicago Art Institute, 8
children, projects for, 93, 108–10
china, design motifs from, 33
Chinese rugs, imitating, 93
clothing, design motifs from, *29*, *30*
color(s), 29
    to accentuate good points, 72
    border stencils and, 26
    for doors, 95
    for floors, 93, 94
    for formal rooms, 71
    to improve awkward features, 72–74
    limiting number of, 59
    mood creation with, 75
    multicolored designs, 20–*23*, 26
    paint, 79–80, 94
    separating, with ties, *18*
    for small rooms, 70, 71
complicated stencils, 13–*16*
cooking, design motifs from, 52
corner treatment, borders and, *84–90*
crescent board, 77

dado, 62, *63*, 74, 79
Deerfield, Massachusetts, 7
Denver Botanical Gardens, 8–*9*, *43*, *75*, *91*
design motifs, 29–60, *111–34*
    adapting, for stenciling, 59–*60*
    from art of other cultures, 53–*57*, 93, 106, 108
    for floorcloths, 108
    for folding screens, 106
    full-size, for tracing, *111–34*
    from household objects, *29–35*
    mood creation with, 75
    in the neighborhood, *41–44*
    from nonsporting amusements, *52–53*
    from reference books, 58, 106
    on sea and land, *45–48*
    from sports, 48–*51*
    in United States, 7–9
    from the yard, *36–40*
Designs and Patterns From Historic Ornament (Audsley), 58
door(s), 95
    borders, 61, 74, *87–90*
    unusual, decorating, 72

Eaton, Moses, 7
enamel paint, 95, 110
equipment for stenciling, 7, 77, 79–81
    for basic design, 11
    on ceilings, 95
    for complicated stencils, 13
    for floorcloths, 108
    for floors, 94
    for folding screens, 106

farms, design motifs from, *44*
field designs, 61, 64–*69*, 72, 74
file cabinet, *96*, 105
finishing wall stencils, 91
fish:
    as design motif, *45–46*
    stencil of, 18, *19*
floorcloths, 108
floors, 93–94
flowerpot variations, *49*
flowers, design motifs from, *36*, 58
folding screen, 105–107
folk art, design motifs from, 53–*57*, 93, 106, 108
furniture, *96*, *105*

gesso, 106, 107, 108, 110
glassware shapes, design motifs from, *33*
graph paper, 15, 77
graph tracing paper, 15, 110
grid patterns, 64–68, 77

horses:
    as design motif, 51
    multicolored, 20–*21*
household objects as design motifs, 29–35
houses, *see also* buildings:
    design motifs from, 38, *39–40*
    multicolored, 22–*23*
Indian art, design motifs from, 53, *55–56*, 58, 93, 108
inlaid wood floors, imitating, 93
insects, design motifs from, 36, *37–38*
Islamic art, 8, 108

Japan:
    family-crest designs of, 53, 56–*57*, 106
    stencils of, 58, 106
Jessop, Jared, 7

kitchen items, design motifs from, *34-35*

latex paints, 81, 95, 105, 107, 108, 110
line, simplicity of, 59
Lipman, Jean, 7
lunchboxes, 110

man-made wonders as design motifs, 48
Mark Twain Memorial, Hartford, Connecticut, *8*, *10*, *78*
medicine chest, *92*
mistakes, correcting, 90
mitered corners, 88, 90
mood, creating a, 72, 75
Mumford, New York, 7
musical instruments, design motifs from, 52

National Geographic, 58
natural wonders as design motifs, *48*
Navajo rugs, imitating, 93, 108
neighborhood, design motifs from, *41-44*
notepaper, 109

oriental rugs, imitating of, 93, 108

paint, 110
   colors, 79-80, 94
   for doors, 95
   for floorcloths, 108
   for floors, 94
   for folding screens, 107
   for furniture, 105
   for window shades, 96
paintbrushes, 81, 106, 107, 108
paper, stenciling on, 108-10
planning of rooms, *61-78*
plants, *see also* flowers:
   design motifs from, *31-32*, *36*, *45*
polybrush, 106, 107, 108
polyurethane varnish, 91, 94, 95, 107, 108
pot design, *28*
projects, *93-110*

radially symmetrical designs, 14-15
Ranger Rick, 58
reference books, design motifs from *58*, 93, 106
regional characteristics, design motifs from, 53
registration, *24*
rooms, planning of, *61-78*
   enhancing good points, 72
   formal and informal, 71
   improving awkward features, *72-74*
   large, 70
   mood creation in, 75
   preliminary sketches, 77
   small, 70-71

scaffolding, 95
screens, folding, 105-107
sculpture, design motifs from, 43
sea, design motifs from the, *45-46*, 48

shading, designs depending upon, 59
Shelburne Museum, Vermont, 7
signs, design motifs from, *41-42*
snake stencil, *18*, *19*
sports, design motifs from, *48-51*
stamps, design motifs from, 52
stencil board, 13, 20, 22-26, 109, 110
   cutting, 15
   transferring design to, 14, 15
stripes, *see* borders and stripes
Sturbridge Village, Massachusetts, 7
Sullivan, Louis, 7, 8
sunburst as border design, *26*
superimposing colors, *22-23*
symmetrical designs, multicolored, *20-21*

table, *105*
ties, stencils with, *17-18*, 59
Tiffany, Louis C., 7, 8
tile floors, imitating, 93, 108
totem poles as design motifs, 56, 81
tracing paper, 15, 110
transportation vehicles, design motifs from, 36, 38, *39*, 41, *43-44*
trellis designs, *68*, 106
T-shirts, 110

United States:
   design motifs from folk art of, 53, *55*, *58*, 106, 108
   history of stenciling in, 5, *7-10*

varnish, 91, 94, 95, 96, 105, 107, 108, 110
vegetables, design motifs from, *36*
vine stencil, 18, *19*, 59, 87

wainscoting, 62, 74, 79
wallpaper designs, 68
wall stenciling, *79-91*
   borders, *84-90*
   supplies, 79-81
   techniques, 81
Waring, Janet, 7
weather, design motifs from, 38, *39-40*
window(s):
   borders, *61*, 74, *87-90*
   decorating unusual, 72
window shades, 96
wrapping paper, 108-109

X-acto knife, 13, 18, 81, 107

yard, design motifs from the, *36-40*